Vocabulary Strategies That Work

Do This—Not That!

D1278136

Lori G. Wilfong, Ph.D.

EYE ON EDUCATION
6 DEPOT WAY WEST, SUITE 106
LARCHMONT, NY 10538
(914) 833-0551
(914) 833-0761 fax
www.eyeoneducation.com

For information about permission to reproduce selections from this book, write

Eye On Education
Permissions Department, Suite 106
6 Depot Way West
Larchmont, New York 10538

Sponsoring Editor: Robert Sickles
Production Editors: Lauren Davis and Lauren Beebe
Copy Editor: Dorothy Anderson
Designer and Compositor: Rick Soldin
Cover Designer: Armen Kojoyian

Library of Congress Cataloging-in-Publication Data

Wilfong, Lori G.
 Vocabulary strategies that work : do this, not that! / Lori G. Wilfong, Ph.D.
     p. cm.
 Includes bibliographical references.
 ISBN 978-1-59667-229-1
1. Vocabulary--Study and teaching (Elementary) I. Title.
 LB1574.5.W55 2012
 372.44--dc23   2012031113

10 9 8 7 6 5 4 3 2 1

Also Available from Eye On Education

Common Core Literacy Lesson Plans:
Ready-to-Use Resources, K–5
Ed. Lauren Davis

Common Core Literacy Lesson Plans:
Ready-to-Use Resources, 6–8
Ed. Lauren Davis

Common Core Literacy Lesson Plans:
Ready-to-Use Resources, 9–12
Ed. Lauren Davis

Big Skills for the Common Core:
Literacy Strategies for the 6–12 Classroom
Amy Benjamin with Michael Hugelmeyer

Reaching English Language Learners in Every Classroom:
Energizers for Teaching and Learning
Debbie Arechiga

Awakening Brilliance in the Writer's Workshop:
Using Notebooks, Mentor Texts, and the Writing Process
Lisa Morris

Teaching Critical Thinking:
Using Seminars for 21st Century Literacy
Terry Roberts and Laura Billings

Vocabulary at the Core:
Teaching the Common Core Standards
Amy Benjamin and John T. Crow

Teaching Grammar: What Really Works
Amy Benjamin and Joan Berger

Contents

Setup of This Book

To describe each item on the **Do This–Not That** list, this text has been set up with a specific structure:

♦ A description of the research behind each "Do This" item

♦ Strategies that update traditional instructional practice for each item on the list

♦ Common Core State Standards that correlate with each strategy

♦ Action steps and reflection items for each item to help spur your instructional change!

Supplemental Downloads

Several of the templates discussed and displayed in this book are also available on Eye On Education's Web site as Adobe Acrobat files. Permission has been granted to purchasers of this book to download these resources and print them.

You can access these downloads by visiting Eye On Education's Web site: www.eyeoneducation.com. From the home page, click on FREE, then click on Supplemental Downloads. Alternatively, you can search or browse our Web site to find this book, then click on "Log in to Access Supplemental Downloads."

Your book-buyer access code is **VTW-7229-1**.

Index of Free Downloads

Meet the Author

Lori G. Wilfong, Ph.D., began her career as a naïve (and yet know-it-all) teacher at a middle school in East Los Angeles. Two days into her job teaching English to 6th, 7th, and 8th grade English language learners, she realized how much she *didn't* know about teaching, and this set the course for the rest of her career, to learn as much as she could about motivating adolescent readers, reading in the content areas, young adult literature, and differentiated instruction. A frenzy of advanced degree-getting followed, including a master's in Reading Specialization and a doctorate in Curriculum & Instruction, both from Kent State University. She worked as a literacy coach and a literacy specialist in rural and urban districts in Northeast Ohio before landing in the department of Teaching, Learning, and Curriculum Studies at Kent State University at Stark, where she is currently an Associate Professor, teaching courses in literacy to both preservice and practicing teachers. Lori continues to hone her skills in school districts, working with teachers with one goal always in mind: to make all students love reading. She has been published in esteemed journals such as the *Reading Teacher, Journal of Adolescent & Adult Literacy, Voices from the Middle*, and *Science Scope*. She lives in Munroe Falls, Ohio, with her husband, Bob.

Foreword

Phonics is not enough! It's clear that students' knowledge of word meaning is critical to their success in reading. What good is it for students to be able to "sound out" a word if they don't know what the word they "sounded out" means? Essentially such words are nonsense words for those readers. A large body of research over the past several decades has shown a consistent relationship between readers' knowledge of word meanings and their ability to comprehend texts (Newton, Padak, & Rasinski, 2007). The problem becomes translating research findings into practical strategies that teachers can use to promote students' vocabulary growth.

In her book *Vocabulary Strategies That Work*, Lori Wilfong has assembled a set of proven instructional strategies that will not only grow students' word knowledge but also their fascination with words. The strategies can easily be integrated into nearly any classroom setting. Moreover, Lori's clear and engaging writing style makes the strategies easily accessible to busy teachers who are looking for ways to add a bit more emphasis into their word-study programs.

Early chapters focus on assessing students' vocabulary knowledge and identifying words that are worth teaching to students. These are followed by chapters that focus on specific ways to make vocabulary instruction work for students. One chapter, for example, focuses on how to use word walls effectively. Nearly every elementary classroom I visit nowadays has one or more word walls on display. However, I rarely see students do much with the word walls. They appear to be nothing more than a classroom decoration. Lori shows teachers just how they (and students) can make important words visible to students and how teachers and students can use word walls to deepen their understanding of words.

One of my favorite chapters is on the use of Greek and Latin roots for word study. This is an area of deep personal and professional interest. I took several years of Latin in high school and found it to be one of the least useful courses I took in my high school curriculum. However, when I began my studies in college, I realized that my Latin courses were some of the most valuable courses I took in high school. I found that many of the academic words I was encountering in my math, science, psychology, sociology and other courses were derived from Latin roots and affixes. I found that my knowledge of Latin helped me figure out the meanings to many challenging academic words. Lori recognizes that the study of Latin and Greek roots does not need to be limited to the high school grades. Students in the elementary grades can begin to explore these letter patterns that are embedded with meaning. She provides the readers with ways to integrate the study of Latin and Greek roots into their curricula.

Word study does not need to be a dreary exercise marked by lists of words that need to be defined and memorized. Classroom-based word study can and should be fun and engaging. Lori Wilfong's book *Vocabulary Strategies That Work* goes a long way to help teachers make the classroom exploration of words worthwhile and fascinating.

Timothy Rasinski
Kent State University

DO THIS	NOT THAT!
1. Select words to teach.	1. Assign long lists of words (six to eight a week is recommended) but never teach about the words selected.
2. Use strategies to engage students in word study.	
3. Help students to come up with their own definitions.	2. Have students look up lists of words in a dictionary, write arbitrary sentences, or copy words multiple times.
4. Assess student use of words in authentic writing and speaking.	
5. Teach students morphological strategies to figure out words they do not know, in addition to context-clue strategies.	3. Have students simply copy definitions.
	4. Give students matching tests that show only memorization of definitions.
6. Use symbols and pictures to help bring vocabulary to life.	5. Tell students to use only context clues to figure out an unknown word.
7. Highlight and use a word wall in classroom instruction.	
8. Use and apply vocabulary words regularly (versus isolated practice).	6. Lack the use of visual cues in the classroom to assist with vocabulary instruction.
9. Allow opportunities for wide reading so students are exposed to words all the time in a variety of books.	7. Lack or misuse a word wall in the classroom.
	8. Spend a large chunk of language arts time working on vocabulary in isolation.
10. Model the use of academic language at all times, setting high expectations for language use.	9. Teach only whole-class books/texts with controlled vocabulary study.
	10. Use "kid" language around students and allow students to speak "kid" back.

Take a look at your vocabulary practices, and based on the list, record the following:

Things I am doing now that need to be updated:	Instructional updates I can use:

What evidence can I provide that I am changing my instructional practices?

_____

_____

_____

_____

_____

_____

_____

_____

_____

_____

_____

_____

Introduction

The idea for this book was born out of a conversation with a very wise associate superintendent of North Olmsted City Schools, Anne Pyros. After a round of meetings with a group of teachers, she expressed her frustration to me about certain classroom literacy practices she sees all the time that she would like to put an end to. "Suppose," she mused to me, "we created a list of these literacy practices that were out of date or not research based and then offered replacement strategies to teachers?" A lightbulb went off in my head. We often tell teachers what *not* to do, but we do not often give reasons these strategies are ineffective or give replacement strategies to improve their instructional practices.

Together, Pyros and I picked a topic, vocabulary, and began to brainstorm the ineffective practices we see in classrooms that need to be replaced: assigning too many words, not creating an effective instructional routine, not modeling the use of good academic language, etc. She then gave me the task of thinking of the research-based strategies to replace these. What we created became the basis of this book, *Vocabulary Strategies That Work: Do This—Not That!* As I piloted each item with a team of intermediate teachers in the district, it became obvious that this clear-cut manner of professional development resonated with teachers; I would present the Do This–Not That principle, we would discuss and try the new strategies, and then we would meet again in a month and discuss their successes and challenges with strategies they had tried in their own classrooms. Over nine months, each item was developed, tested, and finally, written. I can't thank the teachers at Maple Intermediate School enough for their dedication and honest feedback!

The goal of this book is to allow both preservice and practicing teachers an opportunity to examine the vocabulary instruction they have experienced or currently teach and update it to reflect research-based practices. Each chapter gives practical reasons why traditional practices may not work well for today's students and then offers multiple strategies for teachers to try out with their students to improve their own instructional practice. A Common Core connection to each principle is given, as well.

Enjoy the process of updating your vocabulary practice!

Chapter 1

Select Words to Teach

José and I had been at odds over his vocabulary grade all year. With his bright green hair and infectious laugh, he was a leader in the classroom and was curious about growing his knowledge of the English language. However, he simply refused to complete his vocabulary homework of looking up words in the dictionary and then using the words in a sentence. I kept him after class one day: "José, you will continue to get a poor grade in vocabulary if you do not do your vocabulary homework!" He grinned at me and opened his binder. "Miss," he said, shuffling through several sets of papers, "have you seen the number of words I have to do the same exercises with?" He pulled out his weekly lists from math, science, and social studies teachers—all teachers on my seventh-grade team. "I have almost 80 words that you all want me to do the same thing with. Some of these words I know, some of these words I don't, but I can tell you that I ain't looking up 80 words. Have you guys ever thought about cutting these lists down?"

Why This Item Is Important

José was pointing out to me in his direct way the fallacy the middle school I taught at had fallen into. As teachers, we were relying heavily on our textbooks to tell us which words to teach, and in doing so, we were completely inundating our students with words to know. José simply gave up, realizing that there was no way he could learn all those words in one week. The ideal number of words that students can handle cognitively is eight to ten a week for deep teaching (Scott, Jamieson-Noel, & Asselin, 2003); José had almost 80 words to learn!

Textbooks commonly identify several words in either the teacher manual or the student edition that are central to the meaning of the text, yet the thinking behind these selections is not clear. Nagy (2008) points out that publishers don't have a consistent rule for selecting important vocabulary; rather, they go with words that are multisyllabic or repeated in later chapters. While it is easy to rely on textbooks to make this instructional decision, selecting which words to teach is too important for teachers to not give their input into the words they teach; they must consider the diversity of their students, students' background knowledge, and which words are truly central to the reading and learning students are expected to do in the classroom.

The strategies and the research on selecting words join together in this chapter. There are several ways teachers can select words for instruction. The resulting words will differ from the words that students will pick up through conversation and reading; in fact, we know we need to rely on students to participate in several reading opportunities to increase their vocabularies exponentially beyond what we are able to achieve in the classroom (addressed in Chapter 8).

> **Do This–Not That** principle #1: **DO** thoughtfully choose words to teach students; **DON'T** assign long lists predetermined by a textbook or publisher.

Updated Strategy #1: Tiering Words

A good beginning strategy to use when selecting vocabulary is to think about the "tiers" or "levels" of words that educators can identify for instruction. Beck, McKeown, and Kucan (2002) tier words like this:

Tier 1—General

Commonplace; learned from interactions with texts and people

Tier 2—Specialized

Change meaning with context (polysemic)

Tier 3—Technical

Specific to the discipline

Content Area Example: An example of this can be done with words and terms related to Memorial Day, such as *freedom, war, picnic, hot dog, veteran, no school,* and *memorial.* Tiered, they look like this:

Tier 1—General

- hot dog
- no school
- picnic

Tier 2—Polysemic

- freedom
- war
- veteran
- memorial

Tier 3—Content Specific

None

The focus on instruction for these words is on the polysemic words—words that have multiple meanings in different contexts. If I am teaching in a social studies class about Memorial Day, the Tier 2 words are important for me to focus on. I introduce students to their meaning in my class, but I would also have them brainstorm meanings for those words in other contexts, too. Polysemic words allow students to have power over academic language!

Updated Strategy #2: Answering Questions

Fisher and Frey (2011) developed a list of questions to assist teachers in deciding if a certain word is truly worthy of their teaching time.

1.	*Representative*	Is the word critical to understanding?
2.	*Repeatability*	Will it be used again?
3.	*Transportable*	Is it needed for discussions or writing?
4.	*Contextual analysis*	Can students use context to figure out the word?
5.	*Structural analysis*	Can they use structure?
6.	*Cognitive load*	Have I exceeded the number of words they can learn?

Content Area Example: A group of fifth-grade science teachers used this list of questions to analyze the set of words the textbook designated for instruction in the classroom, shown in Figure 1.1 on page 6. The text book had thirty-three words designated for study across five lessons.

Figure 1.1 Words to Teach (Recommended by Textbook)

1. **Lesson 1:** crust mantle atmosphere topographical map inner core relief map hydrosphere outer core landform
2. **Lesson 2:** fault geologists plate tectonics
3. **Lesson 3:** magma island arc volcano composite volcano cinder cone volcano hot spot lava island chain shield volcano
4. **Lesson 4:** magnitude earthquake focus epicenter tsunami
5. **Lesson 5:** floodplain erosion deposition weathering meander sediment glacier

Together, the teachers went through each question, scrutinizing each word for inclusion in a direct vocabulary study the teachers would plan.

Question 1: *Is it critical to understanding?* This question resulted in the most difficult discussion the teachers had. It was hard to figure out if a word was truly central to student learning or was important for understanding the text. The teachers relied heavily on those who had taught this content through this textbook to guide them through the selection of words (shown highlighted in Figure 1.2).

Figure 1.2 Representative Words Critical to Understanding

1. **Lesson 1:** crust mantle atmosphere topographical map inner core relief map hydrosphere outer core landform
2. **Lesson 2:** fault geologists plate tectonics
3. **Lesson 3:** magma island arc volcano composite volcano cinder cone volcano hot spot lava island chain shield volcano
4. **Lesson 4:** magnitude earthquake focus epicenter tsunami
5. **Lesson 5:** Floodplain erosion deposition weathering meander sediment glacier

Question 2: *Will it be used again?* This question was easier for the teachers to work through. They went through the rest of the textbook and then went through a sixth- and seventh-grade science book to see how many of the words popped up again (highlighted in Figure 1.3).

Figure 1.3 Repeatable Words

1. **Lesson 1:** crust mantle atmosphere topographical map inner core relief map hydrosphere outer core landform
2. **Lesson 2:** fault geologists plate tectonics
3. **Lesson 3:** magma island arc volcano composite volcano cinder cone volcano hot spot lava island chain shield volcano
4. **Lesson 4:** magnitude earthquake focus epicenter tsunami
5. **Lesson 5:** floodplain erosion deposition weathering meander sediment glacier

Question 3: *Is it needed for discussions or writing?* Teachers went through the assignments they had students complete in conjunction with this chapter of the textbook and selected words that students would need to prove their comprehension of the chapter (highlighted in Figure 1.4).

Figure 1.4 Transportable Words Used in Assignments

1. **Lesson 1:** crust mantle atmosphere topographical map inner core relief map hydrosphere outer core landform
2. **Lesson 2:** fault geologists plate tectonics
3. **Lesson 3:** magma island arc volcano composite volcano cinder cone volcano hot spot lava island chain shield volcano
4. **Lesson 4:** magnitude earthquake focus epicenter tsunami
5. **Lesson 5:** floodplain erosion deposition weathering meander sediment glacier

Question 4: *Can students use context to figure out the word?* This question proved to be the most surprising in paring down the word lists. Allen (2007) asserts that science and social studies texts are the best for providing context clues for students about what a word means. Important words often have the definitions right there in the sentence, set off by commas. A teacher simply needs to point out and remind students about this text feature. Words highlighted in Figure 1.5 are words that were *not* defined in context—only four!

Figure 1.5 Words Not Defined in Context

1. **Lesson 1:** crust mantle atmosphere topographical map inner core relief map hydrosphere outer core landform
2. **Lesson 2:** fault geologists plate tectonics
3. **Lesson 3:** magma island arc volcano composite volcano cinder cone volcano hot spot lava island chain shield volcano
4. **Lesson 4:** magnitude earthquake focus epicenter tsunami
5. **Lesson 5:** floodplain erosion deposition weathering meander sediment glacier

Question 5: *Can they use structure?* After a quick review of a Greek and Latin roots list and consultation with the language arts teachers, who weave this type of vocabulary instruction into their classrooms, the science teachers combed through the list and found a few words they felt students could find the meaning of using structure (Figure 1.6).

Figure 1.6 Words That Can Be Defined by Their Structure

1. **Lesson 1:** crust mantle atmosphere topographical map inner core relief map hydrosphere outer core landform
2. **Lesson 2:** fault geologists plate tectonics
3. **Lesson 3:** magma island arc volcano composite volcano cinder cone volcano hot spot lava island chain shield volcano
4. **Lesson 4:** magnitude earthquake focus epicenter tsunami
5. **Lesson 5:** floodplain erosion deposition weathering meander sediment glacier

Question 6: *Have I exceeded the number they can learn?* This discussion centered on the amount of time the teachers generally take to teach this chapter, which varied from two to four weeks. The teachers who took four weeks to go through the five lessons felt that the number of words selected did not exceed the cognitive load of the students, but the teachers who moved at a quicker rate realized that the number of words far exceeded the cognitive load of the students.

After completing this strategy, the teachers discussed the results:

"Well," exclaimed one teacher, "I am exhausted! I have never thought so in depth about selecting vocabulary words."

One of her colleagues responded, "But I think I have a better idea of which words I really need to teach. I sort of felt that if the words popped up on two or more of the lists from Questions 1 through 3 and were not able to be figured out using the structure or context clues questions, then I should focus on those." The rest of the team nodded in agreement.

Updated Strategy #3: Utilizing a Knowledge Ratings Chart

If you are having trouble cutting down your list, a Knowledge Ratings Chart is a helpful way of letting the students assist you in selecting which words to teach (Vacca, Vacca, & Mraz, 2011). Using the Knowledge Ratings Chart template (page 126), list the words you intend to do direct instruction on in the left-hand column. Distribute the chart to the students prior to teaching the unit. Ask students to honestly mark down whether they can define a word, have seen/heard a word, or have never encountered a word. If they can define or have some idea of what a word means, ask students to write a few words or draw a picture in the "Prove it" column to show you what they know about the word. Encourage students to take this seriously—it will drive their vocabulary learning for the coming unit! Afterward, compile the data and use it to narrow down your list to the appropriate number of words. This strategy will also direct you to which students may need more background knowledge (differentiation opportunity!) prior to your unit. An example of a Knowledge Ratings Chart in a language arts classroom on the book *The Giver* is shown in Figure 1.7 on page 10.

Figure 1.7 Sample Knowledge Ratings Chart

Words	Can define	Have seen/ heard the word before	Do not know this word	Prove it!
Nurture				
Elder				
Rehabilitation				
Volunteer				
Port				

Updated Strategy #4: Encouraging Vocabulary Self-Selection

Looking for a bit more freedom for your students to select their own vocabulary? Vocabulary Self-Selection (VSS) may be the strategy for you. This strategy is designed to promote student decision making in relation to concepts that need to be learned (Vacca, Vacca, & Mraz, 2011). There are a few steps involved:

1. Divide the class into nominating teams of two to five students. As a team, students pick a word from the text selection they feel is important to emphasize. They should choose one or two backup words, too, so that students can't blame their lack of involvement on someone "stealing" their word!

2. Teams present their word to the class, giving the rationale for its study through the following questions:
   - Where is the word located in the text? What is the context of the word?
   - What do team members think the word means? (The team can use both context and resources to give a student-created meaning.)
   - Why does the team think the class should learn this word?

It is helpful to model this strategy for students by picking a word yourself and answering the rationale questions. A VSS session concludes with the students recording the words chosen for study in a learning log or notebook. You may then use the words chosen in any vocabulary strategies for the remainder of the use of the text.

Common Core Connection

Selecting which words to emphasize in instruction is an important part of the Common Core State Standards for English/Language Arts and for the Literacy Standards for History/Social Studies, Science, and Technical Subjects. The standards that relate to the strategies discussed here are presented in Figure 1.8.

Figure 1.8   English/Language Arts Standards

Grade Level	4	5	6
Standard Addressed	**Language Standard** Acquire and use accurately grade-appropriate general academic and domain-specific words and phrases, including those that signal precise actions, emotions, or states of being (e.g., *quizzed, whined, stammered*) and that are basic to a particular topic (e.g., *wildlife, conservation,* and *endangered* when discussing animal preservation).	**Language Standard** Acquire and use accurately grade-appropriate general academic and domain-specific words and phrases, including those that signal contrast, addition, and other logical relation-ships (e.g., *however, although, nevertheless, similarly, moreover, in addition*).	**Language Standard** Acquire and use accurately grade-appropriate general academic and domain-specific words and phrases; gather vocabulary knowledge when considering a word or phrase important to comprehension or expression.

Grade Level	7	8	9–10
Standard Addressed	**Language Standard** Acquire and use accurately grade-appropriate general academic and domain-specific words and phrases; gather vocabulary knowledge when considering a word or phrase important to comprehension or expression.	**Language Standard** Acquire and use accurately grade-appropriate general academic and domain-specific words and phrases; gather vocabulary knowledge when considering a word or phrase important to comprehension or expression.	**Language Standard** Acquire and use accurately general academic and domain-specific words and phrases, sufficient for reading, writing, speaking, and listening at the college and career readiness level; demonstrate independence in gathering vocabulary knowledge when considering a word or phrase important to comprehension or expression.

Source: (NGAC/CCSSO, 2010)

Action Steps

Selecting which words to emphasize in instruction is not easy! However, the review process can become a time of purposeful curriculum planning. Take some action:

1. List the words the textbook or story designates for emphasis in your instruction:

_____

_____

_____

_____

_____

_____

2. Evaluate each word using the questions from Fisher and Frey (2011):
   a. *Representative*   Is the word critical to understanding?
   b. *Repeatability*   Will it be used again?
   c. *Transportable*   Is it needed for discussions or writing?
   d. *Contextual analysis*   Can students use context to figure out the word?
   e. *Structural analysis*   Can they use structure?
   f. *Cognitive load*   Have I exceeded the number of words they can learn?

3. Were you able to eliminate any words? Which ones? Why?

   _____

   _____

   _____

4. Now, tier your words, using Beck et al. (2002) Tier 1 (everyday), Tier 2 (polysemic), and Tier 3 (content specific) labels.

   Tier 1 words:

   _____

   _____

   Tier 2 words:

   _____

   _____

   Tier 3 words:

   _____

   _____

   Did this help you think about which words to emphasize in your instruction? Why or why not?

   _____

   _____

   _____

   _____

   _____

   _____

5. Create and administer a Knowledge Ratings Chart with your students. Compile the data: which words could the students define, which have they heard/seen, or not heard at all?

_____

_____

_____

_____

_____

_____

_____

6. Now the challenge—try out VSS with your students. What did you think? Did the students identify words of importance? Would you use this again? Why or why not?

_____

_____

_____

_____

_____

Chapter 2

Use Strategies to Engage Students in Word Study

A group of administrators and I recently walked through the intermediate and middle school buildings at a school district. We had been instructed to talk with students quietly about what they were working on to see if they were aware of the focus of instruction for the day. In one particular classroom, the room was silent as students wrote sentences using the words of study. A principal and I stopped next to one young man's desk. He was so engaged in his work that he did not lift his head until I called his name softly. "Jamal, what are you working on today?" He slid his paper over so we could see it. "I am using my vocabulary words in sentences." I looked at his paper. Each word was neatly copied down with the dictionary definition beside it. However, his sentences looked the same:

1. I know what the word bicameral means.
2. I know what the word legislation means.
3. I know what the word veto means.

Why This Item Is Important

A traditional vocabulary classroom often involves students' getting a list of words to study on Monday, looking up words in a dictionary or glossary on Tuesday, writing the words in sentences on Wednesday, playing a game on Thursday, and then taking a test on the words on Friday (Beers, 2002; Ivey & Fisher, 2005). This routine is comfortable and familiar, mostly because this is the routine many teachers had as students. However, many teachers were already wordsmiths as students, readers who loved words. The traditional strategies simply reinforced the word study they already did on their own. To truly create a sense of word study and ownership, teachers need to employ a variety of strategies.

A word about routines: routine is good! For struggling readers, it is often the concrete structure of a routine that supports their learning (Dietz, Hofer, & Fries, 2007). Students who know that at the beginning of each unit of study (not always Monday!) they will select and study different words (chosen through a method learned in Chapter 1, of course) and that these words will be practiced and reinforced through a set routine of strategies avoid the constant re-setting of expectations. Again, we are simply updating our instructional practices.

> **Do This–Not That** principle #2: **DO** engage students in strategies that allow them to manipulate and practice with words; **DON'T** simply assign words to be defined and used in arbitrary sentences as the only experience students will have with words of study.

Updated Strategy #1: Presenting Alike but Different

Compare-and-contrast strategies have been shown to promote growth in student learning by comparing something we already know to something we are learning (Marzano, 2004). In the brain, this physically creates a synapse from the old to the new; the new information finds a way to fit in with what is already known. Allen (2010) has a unique way of presenting a compare-and-contrast activity with vocabulary words, called Alike but Different (Figure 2.1).

Figure 2.1 Alike but Different Weather Words

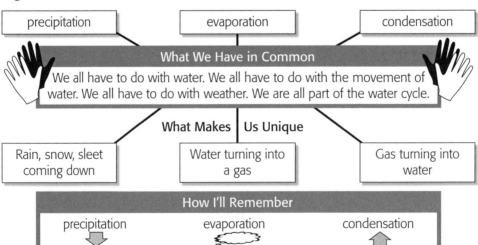

Give students (or allow them to choose) three terms to place in the top three boxes. They then list what these terms have in common and what makes them unique; then they draw a picture or symbol of the words that will help them remember these terms. A blank template of the Alike but Different strategy is located on page 26 for your own use.

Updated Strategy #2: Staging Vocabulary Reader's Theater

This strategy highlights collaborative learning. After students have shown they have some basic knowledge of a word, they work with a partner or partners to practice using the word in correct context to help reinforce what they already know and build upon it. Vocabulary Reader's Theater helps accomplish this. Reader's Theater was developed based on radio plays from the golden age of radio. Actors in these dramas had nothing but their voices to make the scripts come alive. Reader's Theater in a classroom accomplishes the same task, emphasizing prosody (expression) and fluency in readers (Clementi, 2010; Keehn, Harmon & Shoho, 2008). When using this strategy for vocabulary emphasis, give students (or allow them to select) a word of emphasis from the unit. With one or two partners, they write a short script using the word in context. A blank template for this is shown in Figure 2.2 on page 18 (a full-page blank template is on page 27).

To get students started on this strategy, model how to fill out the template. Together, select a word to write about. Show students how to fill out the top, especially emphasizing turning a book definition into a student-friendly definition (explained in Chapter 3). Then show students how to write a mini-play that shows the definition. As students get used to the strategy, it is easy to draft scripts on one day and then share them at appropriate moments in class throughout the week or unit of study. As students advance, instead of telling scripts, they can write riddle scripts, where they give clues about the words. A sample script from eighth-grade social studies is shown in Figure 2.3 on page 19.

Figure 2.2 Vocabulary Reader's Theater

Word: _____

Book definition: _____

_____

Student-friendly definition: _____

_____

Mini-play:

_____

_____

_____

Line 1:

_____

_____

_____

Line 2:

_____

_____

_____

Line 3:

_____

_____

_____

Figure 2.3 Sample Social Studies Script

Line #1:

> I hear the Senate is arguing over an important piece of legislation. It will really affect us if it passes.

Line #2:

> Well, it's a good thing that it goes through the House, too. That way many voices are represented in these important decisions.

Line #3:

> What is this element of our government called?

(The answer is bicameralism.)

Updated Strategy #3: Using Concept Maps

Type "vocabulary concept map" into an Internet search engine, and you get more than half a million hits! This strategy bridges the gap from having students look up words in a dictionary to allowing them to explore the word in a manner that promotes "word learning" not "word memorization" (Beers, 2002). The Frayer Model is a classic example of a concept map. Assign each student a word of emphasis. Students fill out the graphic organizer to explore their words in depth. A blank template of the Frayer Model is in Figure 2.4 (a full-page template is on page 28).

Figure 2.4 Frayer Model

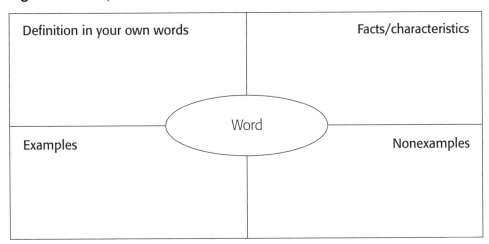

Figure 2.5 Frayer Model of *Quadrilateral*

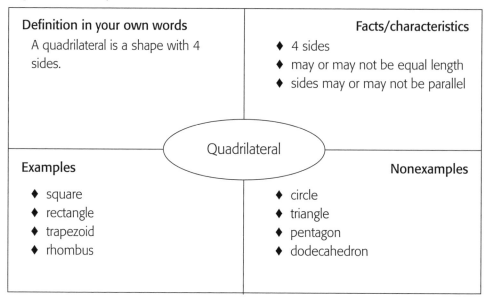

Definition in your own words	Facts/characteristics
A quadrilateral is a shape with 4 sides.	◆ 4 sides ◆ may or may not be equal length ◆ sides may or may not be parallel
Examples ◆ square ◆ rectangle ◆ trapezoid ◆ rhombus	**Nonexamples** ◆ circle ◆ triangle ◆ pentagon ◆ dodecahedron

Going a step beyond traditional vocabulary words, students first define the term in their own words (again, covered in Chapter 3). They then list facts or characteristics about the word. They finish exploring the word by giving examples and nonexamples of the word. Examples should (and could) include a picture or symbol of the word (therefore hitting nonlinguistic representations). A math example is shown in Figure 2.5.

The key with the Frayer Model is to *not* assign an entire list of words for study. It takes most students five to ten minutes to fill out the graphic organizer well, so completing a Frayer Model for an entire list would take too long. Instead, I recommend assigning different words to a table or group of students. Set a timer for students to complete the graphic organizer for their one word and then allow time for them to teach others about their words. To ensure that reciprocal teaching takes place, distribute multiple copies of the Frayer Model, and allow students to take notes from one another.

Updated Strategy #4: Using Semantic Feature Analysis

Like Updated Strategy #1 in this section, Semantic Feature Analysis allows students to compare and contrast words beyond the traditional Venn diagram. However, this strategy in particular allows students to compare Tier 2 words—the words from Chapter 1 that are polysemic, or have multiple meanings. This strategy is especially beneficial for teams of integrated teachers. To begin, identify a word that has one meaning in the classroom and a different meaning in another content area or areas (you may allow students to identify the words). An example comes from a group of eighth graders in a social studies class who were working with the word *base*. They were learning about military bases abroad, and one student was sharing about her time living on a military base in Germany. An English Language Learner raised his hand, a confused look on his face. "So base means something different in here than it does in science?" This is a perfect example of a way to give students power over these words, making it explicit that words can mean one thing in one class or context and something very different in another class or context.

First, the word is presented on a Semantic Feature Analysis Map. You can do this as a whole group on a graphic organizer that you hang where everyone can see and add to it, or you can pass out a paper to students to add to when they find a polysemic word in their reading, as shown in Figure 2.6.

Figure 2.6 Semantic Feature Analysis Map of *Base*

Word	Social Studies	Math	Science	Language Arts/Other
Base				

Students then brainstorm what the word means in these different contexts. They can either draw a picture of what the word means in that context or define the word. The eighth graders just discussed came up with the definitions shown in Figure 2.7 after small group discussions.

Figure 2.7 Semantic Feature Analysis Map of *Base* (Completed)

Word	Social Studies	Math	Science	Language Arts/Other
Base	A place for military operations to take place	A number that is raised to a power	A compound that works with acids to produce a neutral substance	**Baseball**—Places players get to go for different types of hits **Cheerleading**—The person at the bottom of the pyramid

The students surprised the teachers with their "other" definitions, but this creative thinking not only clarified the word for our English Language Learner but allowed students to think about the simple word outside of school, too.

Updated Strategy #5: Building the Chain

The process of thinking about how words relate to each other is important, particularly in the content areas. By allowing students to think of a hierarchy or relationship between the words, they are also building a schema in their minds for how these new words relate to knowledge they already possess. The Chain is a kinesthetic learning strategy that helps students construct this schema.

To use this strategy, write the words being studied on individual note cards as well as on a board or word wall. Hand cards to a variety of students in the classroom. Start this strategy by asking the students with the cards to consider their terms. With the help of their classmates, ask them to identify the central term or terms. Have the student or students with this word or words stand in the center of the classroom. From there, individual students with cards come to the center of the room one by one and arrange themselves around the central term to demonstrate their words' relationship to that term. Each student who joins the chain must give a rationale as to why he or she thinks that word is the next term and where the student is going to place himself or herself—in front of, behind, next to, or even completely separate from the central term. Students build off one another's words until they have a thoughtful and purposeful physical arrangement of the terms. From there, the cards can be placed on the wall in the arrangement the students created, giving them ownership and understanding of how the words are arranged.

Common Core Connection

The strategies presented above fit well with a variety of standards in the Common Core State Standards for English Language Arts and the Literacy Standards for History/Social Studies, Science, and Technical Subjects. They are presented by grade level and content area in Figure 2.8.

Figure 2.8 Common Core State Standards

Grade Level	4	5	6
Standard Addressed	**Reading Standard for Informational Text** Determine the meaning of general academic and domain-specific words and phrases in a text relevant to a *grade 4 topic or subject area.*	**Reading Standard for Informational Text** Determine the meaning of general academic and domain-specific words and phrases in a text relevant to a *grade 5 topic or subject area.*	**Reading Standard for Informational Text** Determine the meaning of words and phrases as they are used in a text, including figurative, connotative, and technical meanings.

Grade Level	4	5	6
Standard Addressed	**Language Standard** Determine or clarify the meaning of unknown and multi-ple-meaning words and phrases based on *grade 4 reading and content,* choosing flex-ibly from a range of strategies. **Language Standard** Demonstrate under-standing of words by relating them to their opposites (antonyms) and to words with sim-ilar but not identical meanings (synonyms).	**Language Standard** Determine or clarify the meaning of unknown and multi-ple-meaning words and phrases based on *grade 5 reading and content,* choosing flex-ibly from a range of strategies. **Language Standard** Use the relationship between particular words (e.g., synonyms, antonyms, homo-graphs) to better understand each of the words.	**Language Standard** Determine or clarify the meaning of unknown and multi-ple-meaning words and phrases based on *grade 6 reading and content,* choosing flex-ibly from a range of strategies. **Language Standard** Use the relationship between particular words (e.g., *cause/ effect, part/whole, item/ category*) to better understand each of the words.

Grade Level	7	8	9–10
Standard Addressed	**Reading Standard for Informational Text** Determine the meaning of words and phrases as they are used in a text, including figura-tive, connotative, and technical meanings; analyze the impact of a specific word choice on meaning and tone. **Language Standard** Determine or clarify the meaning of unknown and multi-ple-meaning words and phrases based on *grade 7 reading and con-tent,* choosing flexibly from a range of strategies. **Language Standard** Use the relationship between particular words (e.g., *synonym/ antonym, analogy*) to better understand each of the words.	**Reading Standard for Informational Text** Determine the meaning of words and phrases as they are used in a text, including figura-tive, connotative, and technical meanings. **Language Standard** Determine or clarify the meaning of unknown and multi-ple-meaning words or phrases based on *grade 8 reading and content,* choosing flexibly from a range of strategies. **Language Standard** Use the relationship between particular words to better under-stand each of the words.	**Reading Standard for Informational Text** Determine the meaning of words and phrases as they are used in a text, including figura-tive, connotative, and technical meanings; analyze the cumulative impact of specific word choices on meaning and tone (e.g., how the language of a court opinion differs from that of a newspaper).

Content Area	Social Studies	Science
Standard Addressed	Determine the meaning of words and phrases as they are used in a text, including vocabulary specific to domains related to history/social studies.	Determine the meaning of symbols, key terms, and other domain-specific words and phrases as they are used in a specific scientific or technical context relevant to *grades 6–8 texts and topics.* Analyze the structure of the relationships among concepts in a text, including relationships among key terms (e.g., *force, friction, reaction force, energy*).

Source: (NGAC/CCSSO, 2010)

Action Steps

These five strategies just scratch the surface of what is out there for engaging, effective vocabulary strategies! Take some action:

1. Most teachers like to start with the third strategy introduced, the Frayer Model. Design a lesson sequence in which you model how to use the graphic organizer as a whole class with a word of emphasis. Then allow students to fill out a template themselves on one or two words. Finally, jigsaw students so that groups of students with different words can teach one another about their words of study.

    a. REFLECT: How did you feel about this strategy? Do you think students learned deeply about the words? Compare the strategy to traditional definition look-up—what do you think?

    _____

    _____

    _____

    _____

    _____

    _____

2. Try out another strategy after you use the Frayer Model. Design a lesson sequence in which you model either Vocabulary Reader's Theater or Alike but Different.

    a. REFLECT: Which strategy did you choose? Why? Would you do it again? What evidence can you give that your students grew through your use of this strategy?

_____

_____

_____

_____

_____

Alike but Different

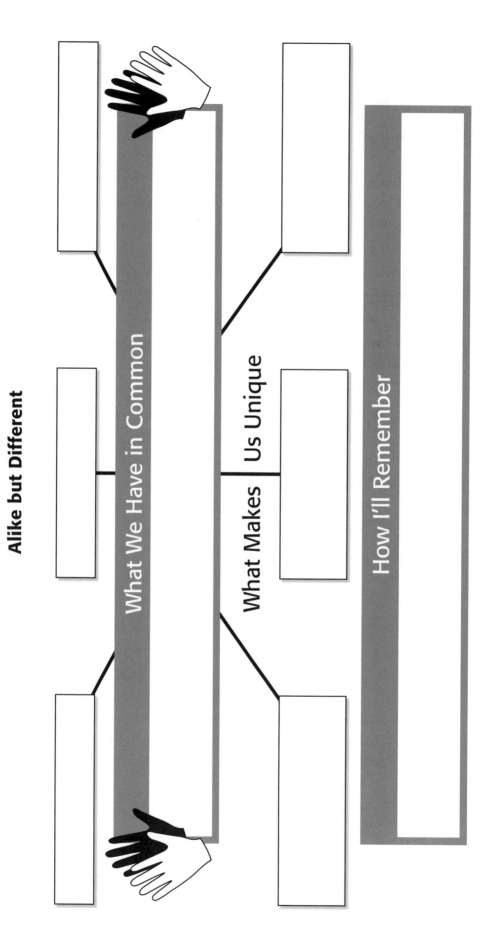

What We Have in Common

What Makes | Us Unique

How I'll Remember

Vocabulary Reader's Theater

Name: _____ Date:_____

With a partner:

♦ Look up the definition of your word. Write it in the book definition box.

♦ Come up with your own "student-friendly" definition. It MUST be three words or fewer. Write it in the student-friendly definition box.

♦ Write a three-line mini-play to help your classmates remember what your word is about.

Word: _____

Book definition: _____

_____

Student-friendly definition: _____

Mini-play:

_____

_____

_____

_____

Line 1:

_____

_____

Line 2:

_____

_____

Line 3:

_____

_____

Frayer Model

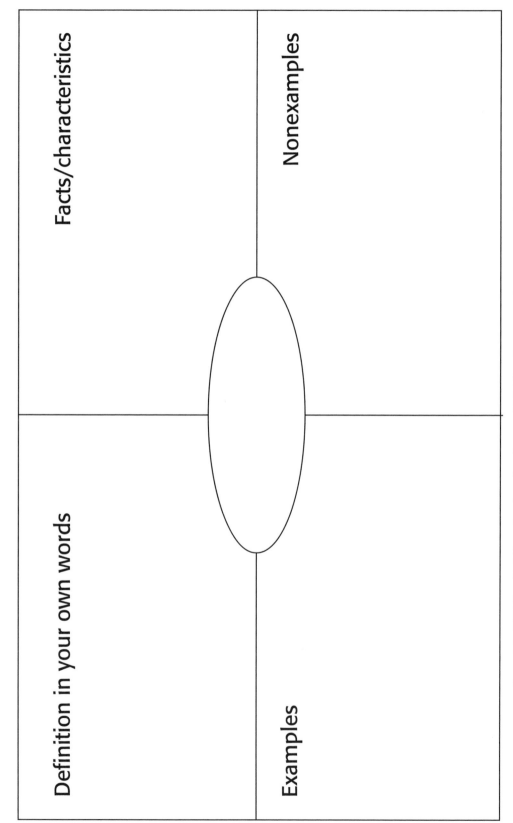

Definition in your own words

Facts/characteristics

Examples

Nonexamples

Chapter 3

Help Students Come Up with Their Own Definitions

As I walked into the ninth-grade language arts classroom, the only sound I could hear was my shoes on the floor. The students' heads were bent intently over their work, while pens and pencils wrote furiously in notebooks. The teacher got up from her desk and gestured grandly at the classroom. "We are working on vocabulary," she said, indicating the massive dictionaries out on the desks. "The students are looking up definitions from the words in their story this week from the anthology." She showed me a long list from the book. "It will probably take all period." I sat down next to a student hard at work. She raised her head. "What are you working on?" I asked, following the protocol from the walk-through sheet the administration had given me. She shrugged her shoulders, "My handwriting, I guess." She lowered her head and went back to copying definitions out of the dictionary.

Why This Item Is Important

The scene that played out in the ninth-grade classroom described above is not isolated to this school on this day. Day after day, teachers ask students to define long lists of words using a dictionary. Chapter 1 discussed how to select important words to teach. Chapter 2 gave strategies to enliven vocabulary study in the classroom. Now we will answer the basic question: how do teachers help students learn the meanings? Looking up a word in a dictionary and copying the definition, a student does exactly what the student on page 29 described—practices handwriting and copying skills. For many students, this becomes a simple, brainless activity, where little thought or attention is given to the actual definition of the word. Vocabulary practice is busywork in the worst sense of the word—students are quiet and working, as depicted at the start of the chapter, but little learning is actually taking place. Studies have proven the ineffectiveness of dictionary definitions as the best tool for word study (Scott & Nagy, 1997) or even having an impact on student reading comprehension (Baumann, Kame'enui, & Ash, 2003).

Teachers may argue in favor of dictionary skills, and I do not deny that the ability to use a dictionary or another reference material is still a strength of a good reader and writer. In fact, the Common Core State Standards for English Language Arts include at least one standard across grade levels about possessing the ability to use reference materials to assist in the learning process. It is what comes next that is important. How can teachers take the idea of copying definitions neatly to the level of assimilation and ownership of new and valuable words?

> **Do This–Not That** principle #3: **DO** encourage students to learn definitions of new words in a way that is meaningful to them; **DON'T** simply assign a long list and allow them to copy the definition straight out of the dictionary.

Updated Strategy #1: Shrinking the Definition

A first step in helping break the student (and the teacher!) from the grip of the dictionary definition is to challenge students to shrink dictionary or glossary definitions down to three words or fewer. Three is somewhat arbitrary; if the list you give students has some robust words, you can always lengthen the maximum number of words in their created definitions to a number that suits you (although I think more than five defeats the purpose of this strategy).

To model this strategy for students, first show a word found in context in a text and then project its extended dictionary definition as shown here:

> **SWAGGER:** Walk or behave in a very confident and typically arrogant or aggressive way; strut; brag; prance

To show students how to read each definition, try to find the definition that fits most closely with the context of the sentence chosen. This sentence is from *The Highest Tide*, by Jim Lynch (2005), and reads, "He had none of his daylight swagger." Think aloud the process: "I don't think the character is strutting or prancing, even walking in a confident way. I do think he is behaving in a confident way." Then place this definition into the Concept Map you are using for initial look-up (from Chapter 2) or into a personal dictionary, emphasizing that there is no point in copying down the rest of the definitions since students are interested in this context of the word. If you are using the Concept Map, have students move on to the other parts of the graphic organizer (sentence and sketch) before moving on to another word.

This strategy takes practice, especially when the definitions are long and arduous. I have watched English language learners look up every word of a definition only to be more confused than when they began. Dictionaries really work only for proficient readers, who are adept at reading, rejecting, and ultimately accepting definitions that are appropriate for the context being studied. There are some great children's dictionaries available, both in print and in electronic formats, that may be more helpful to struggling readers. However, at the upper grades, these dictionaries may lack the depth and breadth of words necessary for students to look up the words.

Something else I emphasize with teachers with this strategy is that the words are always connected to a context or text. Giving the students a list of words to define without any background knowledge of the text or the context from which they come is like trying to find your way somewhere new without a map; you might have a general sense of the direction in which you are going, but ultimately, you need something to help you find your way. The connection to text grounds the words in purpose and meaning.

A final word on this strategy: in Chapter 1, you learned you need to limit the number of words you teach; you also have to limit the number of words you ask students to look up. Assigning groups of students particular words to look up and then having them jigsaw to teach other new words is a meaningful way to provide peer accountability of word meanings. The goal is to teach students to learn to use a dictionary and create definitions on their own; adults rarely are given a list of words to learn before starting a new book. Instead, they use a dictionary occasionally, when need propels them to. By learning to create or shorten definitions to match the purpose of the word in text, you are scaffolding an important skill for your students.

Updated Strategy #2: Building Background

Updated strategy #1 describes the conundrum of the struggling reader and the dictionary—sometimes the student's vocabulary learning turns into a cycle of look up, look up, and look up some more instead of finding answers! How frustrating for a beginning English speaker! In many cases, teachers have to evaluate their use of the dictionary and their reason for having students look up definitions: do you want students to learn dictionary skills, or do you want them to simply begin to understand the word in order to be able to comprehend the text? If the latter is the case, then that is where you need to do some more work to help your students.

Jen, an English Language Learner resource teacher in northeastern Ohio, works with her mainstream counterparts to accommodate her students in their classrooms. "In most subjects," she says, "having the students look up the words would be like torture." To combat this, she started creating simple PowerPoint slides with the focus words for the chapter or text they would be reading. At first, she printed out the slides for only her students as a quick reference sheet. But when she noticed their seatmates looking at the sheets for guidance, she started showing the PowerPoint slides to the entire class at the beginning of the day. Her mainstream social studies counterpart commented on this, "It was like a lightbulb went on for many of these students," she said. "All of a sudden, everyone had a common reference point for the words or concepts that we thought only the ELLs would struggle with. Well, it turned out, everyone was struggling with these words."

Sheltered Instructional Observation Protocol (SIOP) theory suggests that strategies that were initially developed with ELLs in mind are often beneficial for everyone (McLaughlin, 2010). These strategies are often good literacy practices, and the practice of giving students a visual to connect with new vocabulary can be crucial for building background knowledge when reading about a new topic.

To create your own vocabulary background builder, first preview the text to be read *for that day only*. Although previewing the important words for an entire chapter or unit can provide a nice introduction, it can also provide too many words and cognitive overload. Instead, identify the key concepts or terms that will appear in that day's reading. Using PowerPoint or another presentation software, place the word centrally on the slide. Find a picture or graphic to accompany the word. You must next make an instructional decision: display the definition or don't display the definition? Each teacher differs; I know several who display a truncated definition (three words or fewer) just to give the readers an extra boost, while others like just a picture. Figure 3.1 is an example from a science unit about rocks and minerals.

Figure 3.1 Truncated Definition

GEOLOGIST

Person who studies rocks

What happens next is also an instructional decision—some teachers like to show their brief slide show before students read to quickly introduce the important words of the text to the students and then leave the slide show on the screen or pass out copies of the slides so that as students are reading, they have this sheet as a reference guide. Other teachers use the slides in a more directed reading way: they guide students to read a page or two and have the slides projected as the students read so they can use them as needed during reading. I find a combination of the two works well; I briefly present the slides to students for frontloading and then project them as a slide show while students are reading.

The word *brief* appears twice in the previous paragraph for one reason: this strategy should not take oodles of time. This is a time to do direct instruction on the vital vocabulary of the reading, not engage students in lengthy discussion about each word and its multiple meanings. When Jen, the ELL instructor, uses this strategy in classrooms, she simply projects the slides, pronounces the words carefully for the students, and then points to the picture and tells the word's meaning. More meaningful conversation takes place about the words when students engage in word study, using strategies like those given in Chapter 2.

Common Core Connection

Encouraging students to use reference materials is included in the Common Core State Standards for English Language Arts and the Literacy Standards for History/Social Studies, Science, and Technical Subjects, as shown in Figure 3.2 on page 34.

Figure 3.2 Common Core State Standards

Grade Level	4	5	6
Standard Addressed	**Reading Standard for Informational Text** Determine the meaning of general academic and domain-specific words and phrases in a text relevant to a *grade 4 topic or subject area.* **Language Standard** Use context (e.g., definitions, examples, or restatements in text) as a clue to the meaning of a word or phrase. Consult reference materials (e.g., dictionaries, glossaries, thesauruses), both print and digital, to find the pronunciation and determine or clarify the precise meaning of key words and phrases.	**Reading Standard for Informational Text** Determine the meaning of general academic and domain-specific words and phrases in a text relevant to a *grade 5 topic or subject area.* **Language Standard** Use context (e.g., cause/effect relationships and comparisons in text) as a clue to the meaning of a word or phrase. Consult reference materials (e.g., dictionaries, glossaries, thesauruses), both print and digital, to find the pronunciation and determine or clarify the precise meaning of key words and phrases.	**Reading Standard for Informational Text** Determine the meaning of words and phrases as they are used in a text, including figurative, connotative, and technical meanings.

Source: (NGAC/CCSSO, 2010)

Action Steps

Finding the right time to use dictionaries to define words is a balancing act. Students need to learn how to make dictionary definitions their own by creating or shrinking down long definitions to manageable bites, while teachers have to take responsibility for words by frontloading and scaffolding while learning. Good readers know that a variety of context clue types are available to help them learn unknown words; mastery of these types will lead to confidence in figuring out word definitions on their own. Take some action:

1. Have students practice shrinking dictionary definitions down to three words or fewer (or whatever works for you). Design a lesson sequence in which you model shrinking a dictionary definition to your decided number of words. This strategy is built into the Vocabulary Reader's Theater in Chapter 2 (see template on page 27).

    a. Give students a small number of words to practice on, along with a text they are currently reading.

    b. Have students with the same words compare their truncated definitions with one another—did they come up with the same definitions?

    c. Have students who studied different words share their definitions with one another.

    d. REFLECT: How well did your students shrink the definitions to the designated number of words? Were they able to focus in on the key words necessary to define each word?

    _____

    _____

    _____

    _____

    _____

2. Frontload students with definition/image PowerPoint slides. Which words are vital to their reading and learning?

    _____

    _____

    _____

    _____

    _____

Chapter 4

Assess Student Use of Words in Authentic Writing and Speaking

A precocious eighth grader once described her weekly vocabulary test to me like this: "I get my list of words on Monday. I write the words on note cards, with their definitions on the back. I quiz myself during the week to make sure that I memorized the meaning. I take the matching test on Friday. Over the weekend, the meanings of the words ooze out of my ear, and then I start the whole process again the following week." When I asked her if she remembers any of the words and their meanings, she shrugged and said, "I remember a couple, but I almost never need them again. I learn them for the test; that's it."

Why This Item Is Important

Gallagher (2009) describes a recipe for killing the joy of reading for adolescent learners:

Kill-a-reader Casserole

- ✓ Take one large novel.
- ✓ Dice into as many pieces as possible.
- ✓ Douse with sticky notes.
- ✓ Remove book from oven every five minutes and insert worksheets.
- ✓ Add more sticky notes.
- ✓ Baste until novel is unrecognizable, far beyond well done.
- ✓ Serve in choppy, bite-sized chunks.

I would add, "Quiz students on vocabulary from reading every chapter or so, with matching and multiple choice tests." I am as guilty as the next teacher in doing this during my time as a middle school teacher. The teacher's guide that accompanied many novels and stories I read with my students came with a list of vocabulary for students to learn and often provided short quizzes to test their vocabulary knowledge, too. These quizzes were most likely matching tests, with a few multiple choice items thrown in for good measure. But what was I really assessing? Fisher and Frey (2008) make a strong case for what I was *not* assessing: breadth and depth. They assert that most quizzes "isolate" words, when in reality, the real knowledge of a word comes from being able to relate it to other words and know its multiple meanings. Expanding our view of how to assess vocabulary allows students to demonstrate their ownership of a word beyond the traditional views, essentially showing us their breadth and depth of vocabulary knowledge.

> **Do This—Not That** principle #4: **DO** assess students' vocabulary knowledge through oral discussion, connected writing, and a variety of strategies; **DON'T** use only multiple choice and/or matching items as assessment.

There are two ways for students to show what they know about vocabulary (Stahl & Bravo, 2010):

1. Receptive vocabulary: Students demonstrate they can understand what a word means when they encounter it while listening or reading. Graphic organizers and typical standardized test items are examples of these assessments.

2. Productive vocabulary: Students apply and use new words when writing or speaking. Domain-specific writing and peer discussion are examples of these assessments.

To Get Started

Wiggins and McTighe (2005) explain that teachers should begin with the end in mind. When instructing students in vocabulary across content areas, think about what exactly you want students to do with their new knowledge. For example, in science, should students be able to use the language of the domain in a lab report? In math, should students working with a partner to answer a story problem talk about the correct steps in a process? Rarely would teachers say that they want students to be able to correctly identify a definition in isolation; rather, teachers want their students to sound like practitioners of the subject they are studying, either in speech or in writing.

Developing a framework for assessment clarifies expectations for both you and the students. How often will you assess them on their vocabulary development? Will the assessments be formative or summative in nature? Answers to these questions are individual, so a few suggestions follow:

♦ Use both formative and summative assessments to assess vocabulary development. Formative assessments allow you to track progress on a daily or weekly basis, allowing instruction to be modified to accommodate student growth appropriately. Use summative assessments at the end of a unit or chapter to see what growth a student has made over a longer period of time.

♦ Address both the speaking and writing domains in vocabulary assessments. Many students develop oral proficiency in new vocabulary first; by assessing this (often formatively) you validate their use of a new word before they transfer the word to their writing.

♦ Assessing vocabulary does not have to be through a formal test. Correct completion of graphic organizers and vocabulary strategies are strong indicators of vocabulary development (Fisher, Brozo, Frey, & Ivey, 2011; McKenna & Robinson, 2009).

Keeping these tips in mind, think about your framework in terms of numbers: Use two formative assessments, one oral and one graphic organizer, over the course of a unit? Use one oral formative assessment? Use one summative assessment at the end of the unit? Include a few vocabulary items on a summative assessment related to vocabulary? Decide what is best for your students and the learning outcomes you expect.

Updated Strategy #1: Using the Oral Domain for Assessing Vocabulary

Oral use of a word leads to incrementality (Pearson, Hiebert, & Kamil, 2007); every time students encounter or use a word, they are increasing their capacity to use the word effectively. Student use of a word can be measured both formally and informally.

Formative Assessment. One way to scaffold use of academic language in discussion is through the use of Think-Pair-Share (Vacca, Vacca, & Mraz, 2011). This traditional discussion strategy allows students to formulate answers to questions posed by the teacher and then practice answers with a partner before reporting to the class. I like to take this strategy to a new level with a graphic organizer (Figure 4.1, page 40). A full-size template is available on page 53.

Figure 4.1 Think-Pair-Share

Question or prompt	What I thought	What my partner thought	What we will share

To facilitate the use of academic language with this strategy, explicitly explain that students must include the language of the discipline in their written responses. Just as important is your question or prompt; it must be written in such a way as to promote the use of academic language. Modeling of these expectations is imperative to produce the desired results.

To measure this discussion, use a simple checklist to show progress in student use of the targeted vocabulary. Record the date and the words used in a roster. Assign points to each word used correctly, and make students aware that you are listening for their use of the appropriate vocabulary (so many points for so many words).

Summative Assessment. Presentations provide an opportunity for you to assess students on their use of academic vocabulary. Presentations can take on a variety of formats in various content areas: debates, biographies, formal explanations, etc. To facilitate the assessment of their language in these presentations, present to students prior to their performance a rubric that includes a line item that specifically addresses vocabulary. A generic rubric criterion to measure this is shown in Figure 4.2.

Figure 4.2 Vocabulary Rubric

	3	2	1
Academic language in presentation	Student correctly includes several important vocabulary terms that enhance the presentation.	Student includes some vocabulary terms that clarify the presentation.	Student includes few vocabulary terms in the presentation.

Again, to facilitate this activity, model expectations, provide times during class for students to practice their use of academic language, and be clear when assigning this presentation that certain vocabulary is expected. You might even include a list of words that students could use in their presentation. For example, in a sixth-grade science classroom, one teacher gave her students a list of the important vocabulary terms covered in a textbook chapter for students to include in a news team presentation. She then evaluated her students on their correct usage of these terms in their news reports (Wilfong, 2012).

Updated Strategy #2: Using Contextual Writing and Reading to Assess Vocabulary

Context is key when you assess vocabulary through reading and writing tasks (Miller & Veatch, 2011). Context makes the application of a word authentic. Some standardized testing items do an adequate job at presenting words in context, such as in Figure 4.3.

Figure 4.3 Vocabulary Assessment Through Context

Read the following sentence:

First he stirred fresh mint leaves with sugar and secret ingredients in a small pot on the stove for a very long time, concocting a fragrant elixir of mint.

The word "concocting" means:

A. Examining

B. Creating

C. Imagining

D. Tasting

These types of items can be used both formatively and summatively as a quick exit slip to see if students are starting to grasp important terms and on more formal assessments as measurements of key words. Teachers often use these assessment items because they are easy to create and find (using state databases of released test items).

The cloze procedure is another easily created assessment item you can use for both pre- and post-assessment and for both comprehension and vocabulary. Select a paragraph from a content area text, leaving the first and last sentences and all punctuation in place. Then replace key terms with blanks, placing the deleted terms in a word bank. Students read the passage and fill in the blanks with words from the word bank. A math example of a cloze test is shown in Figure 4.4 on page 42.

Figure 4.4 Cloze Procedure

Directions: Use the vocabulary in the Word Bank to complete the paragraph.

Word Bank

called   equations   careful
equivalent   operation

What Is an Equivalent Equation?

In an equation, the two sides need to balance. So to solve an equation, you

must be _____ to keep that balance by performing the same

_____ on each side of the equation. When two _____

have the same set of solutions they are _____ equivalent equa-

tions. For example, the equations x=5 and x−5=0 are _____.

They have only one solution—the number 5

Answers:
1. careful
2. operation
3. equations
4. called
5. equivalent

(Miller & Veatch, 2011)

Figure 4.5 Concept Maze

Directions: The paragraph below has four words missing. Under each blank space are three possible choices. Circle the word that best completes each sentence.

Forming Equivalent Equations

In an equation, the two sides need to _____. So to solve
<small>reduce, balance, solve</small>
an equation, you must be careful to keep that balance by performing the
same _____ on each side of the equation. When two
<small>operation, number, subtraction</small>
equations have the same set of solutions, they are equivalent. For example,
the equations x = 5 and x − 5=0 are _____. They have
<small>irrational, inverse, equivalent</small>
only one _____ —the number 5.
<small>slope, ratio, solution</small>

(Ketterlin-Geller et al., 2006)

A modification of the cloze procedure is the concept maze (Ketterlin-Geller, McCoy, Twynman, & Tindal, 2006). Instead of removing words and placing them in a word bank, as you do in a cloze test, you insert blanks for key terms and then ask students to choose from three terms for each blank to fill in the correct term. This measures academic language specific to the subject being studied. An example of this type of cloze is shown in Figure 4.5.

Writing in the content areas provides many opportunities to assess students' command of academic language. Lab reports in science, document-based responses in social studies, rationales for answers in math, and essays in language arts are all examples of writing on which students can be evaluated on their use of vocabulary. The key to making this an assessment item is construction of a criterion on a rubric that specifically addresses the students' use of the appropriate vocabulary. An example of a rubric item for science vocabulary in a lab report is shown in Figure 4.6.

Figure 4.6 Science Vocabulary Rubric

	Exceeding the Standard	Meeting the Standard	Approaching the Standard	Not Meeting the Standard
Use of academic vocabulary	Student accurately uses all appropriate scientific vocabulary.	Student accurately uses most appropriate scientific vocabulary.	Student accurately uses some appropriate scientific vocabulary.	Student uses no appropriate scientific vocabulary or does not use it accurately.

When explaining *appropriate scientific vocabulary* to students, you might quantify what scientific vocabulary you mean for a particular lab report by providing a required list or even going as far as to say how many words you expect.

Constructed Response Questions. This excellent type of writing assessment can be used across content areas to measure cognitive skills and content knowledge. These types of questions often start with a simple question (What is the purpose of bartering?) and then build to more complex, analytical questions (What effect did Lewis and Clark have on the economies of the Native Americans they encountered on their expedition?). These types of questions are easy to evaluate for academic language; again, a criterion on the rubric must refer to the vocabulary that is expected of the students. A sample line item on a rubric for this type of question referring only to vocabulary usage is shown in Figure 4.7 on page 44.

Figure 4.7 Sample Vocabulary Rubric

	3	**2**	**1**
Use of vocabulary	Student uses appropriate vocabulary of the discipline to explain answer.	Student uses both appropriate vocabulary of the discipline and everyday terms to explain answer.	Student uses mostly everyday terms to explain answer.

Setting, modeling, and clearly explaining expectations on these types of assessments is important.

Writing Frames. These can be a helpful way to scaffold this type of academic writing with vocabulary for students (Fisher & Frey, 2008). Writing frames allow students to borrow the language of academic experts as they work toward incorporating this vocabulary on their own. Frames can be used at either the sentence level or the paragraph level. I often explain frames to students as the backbone; students are responsible for filling in the muscle. Fisher and Frey offer a great example for helping students support a claim in any content area, shown in Figure 4.8.

Figure 4.8 Argumentative Claim Writing Frame

The argument that _____ is supported by _____,

_____ and _____. For example,

_____ shows that _____.

Argumentative Writing Frame Completed in Language Arts about the Hunger Games trilogy

The argument that Katniss really loved Peetah is supported by the emptiness she felt when he did not want to be part of her life in the second book and that she ended up marrying him in the end of the third book. For example, the fact that she takes the rejection from Gale in stride shows that she is falling in love with Peetah.

Source: Fisher & Frey, 2008

Figure 4.9 has two great electronic resources for writing frames.

Figure 4.9 Electronic Sources for Writing Frames

Type of Frame	Web site
Discussion Frame	www.readingonline.org/articles/art_index. asp?HREF=writing/index.html
Compare & Contrast Frame	www.k8accesscenter.org/writing/writingframes.asp

Updated Strategy #3: Using Strategies and Graphic Organizers to Assess Vocabulary

Knowledge Ratings Chart as Assessment. Chapter 1 discussed the Knowledge Rating Chart: students at the beginning of a unit or chapter help inform instruction by filling out a chart indicating if a word is new to them, if they have an idea what the word is about, or if they are able to draw or write a definition of a word. To turn this into an assessment, modify the choices in the chart slightly (Stahl & Bravo, 2010), as shown in Figures 4.10 and 4.11 on page 46.

Figure 4.10 Original Knowledge Ratings Chart from Chapter 1

Words	Can define	Have seen/ heard the word before	Do not know this word	Prove it!
Nurture				
Elder				
Rehabilitation				
Volunteer				
Port				

Figure 4.11   Modified Knowledge Ratings Chart for Assessment

Words	Definition of word as it relates to book	Context of word	Picture of word (if desired)
Nurture			
Elder			
Rehabilitation			
Volunteer			

With slightly modified labels on the columns, students are able to demonstrate how they have learned the words as they relate to the reading. This can be a quick formative assessment as students gain new word knowledge over the course of a reading, or it can be a summative assessment at the end of a unit or chapter with more terms.

Word Sorts as Assessment. Word sorts can be an effective pre- and post-test, allowing students to demonstrate word knowledge through their manipulation of words into categories based on meaning. More importantly, students are able to show their knowledge of relationships among words (Fisher et al., 2011). Word sorts are generally set up with the teacher providing a set of words on individual slips of paper. Students manipulate the words into logical groupings, depending on the topic being studied (for example, fruits or vegetables in health, attributes of landforms in social studies, geometry versus algebra words in math). Sorts can be set up in two different ways, depending on the teacher's goal.

1. **Closed Sort:** In this type of word sort, you provide the categories into which the student sorts the words. This is an effective pre- or post-unit because you are able to see what misconceptions a student has prior to teaching a unit. To assess their learning of the words over the course of the unit, you can administer the same sort at the end so students can demonstrate their mastery of sorting these terms into their correct categories. Figure 4.12 is an example of a closed sort.

Figure 4.12 Example of a Closed Sort in Language Arts

Sort the following words into the correct type of noun:
Proper   Common   Pronoun
I   Cleveland   me   bike   Colina   intermediate
you   river   Mickey Mouse   San Diego   stapler

2. **Open Sort:** In this type of word sort, the students create their own categories for sorting the words. This type of sort often reflects higher-level thinking; the categories created can show students' knowledge not only of the concepts but also of the relationships between them. Open sorting does allow for assessment; as a pre-assessment, it allows you to see what a student does or does not know about a topic being studied. As a post-assessment, an open sort shows you how the students apply the knowledge they gained over the course of a unit to create logical categories. Open sorts are challenging to some students, especially when learning the strategy. An example of the challenge lies in giving the students the freedom to choose their categories; a school district that used sorts as students learn new Greek and Latin roots was frustrated at the number of students who simply put the words in alphabetical order instead of sorting them into categories. A whole-group sort to model the kinds of thinking the teacher expects during this activity can help alleviate some of these misconceptions. Many interactive whiteboard programs allow teachers to model how to do an open sort. To amp up the assessment features of open sorts, students can write a rationale to explain their sorting categories (Fisher & Frey, 2008). Figure 4.13 is an example of an open sort.

Figure 4.13 Example of an Open Sort in Social Studies (Civil War Unit)

Sort the following words into categories that make sense to you. After you are finished sorting, label your categories and provide a rationale for your organization.
Battle of Antietam   Emancipation Proclamation   Dixie   rebels Underground Railroad   Abraham Lincoln   Stonewall Jackson plantation   cotton   Gettysburg   Jefferson Davis   Fort Sumter

Sorts allow for opportunities for reteaching. If a student creates a category on a sort for "Words I Don't Know," you can individualize specific instruction on that word or words for students or small groups of students.

Figure 4.14 Semantic Feature Analysis of Italian Cuisine

	Is a type of pasta	Is a dessert	Is stuffed with meats and cheeses	Can be baked
Ravioli				
Spaghetti				
Lasagna				
Fettuccini				
Tiramisu				

Semantic Feature Analysis as Assessment. Chapter 2 examined several strategies for engaging students in polysemic words across that span of content areas. Semantic feature analysis can also be a way to see student knowledge about characteristics of words both pre- and post-unit.

To set up a semantic feature analysis in a single content area on a unit of study, you must list important terms. For example, a lesson on Italian cuisine might include *ravioli, spaghetti, lasagna, fettuccini,* and *tiramisu.* Next, brainstorm a list of characteristics these foods *might* have. Some foods might have one of the characteristics; others might have all or none. Present the terms and characteristics in a table like the one shown in Figure 4.14.

Students put a check mark in the characteristic that applies to the term. As a pre-assessment, the semantic analysis allows you to see what knowledge a student already has on a subject; as a post-assessment, it allows you to see what characteristics a student has learned about a variety of terms.

As students become proficient at completing semantic feature analyses, they can begin to create their own about topics of study!

A–Z Lists as Assessment. Another great pre- or post-assessment, A–Z lists, follow a KWL format: students begin a unit by brainstorming all the words they know about a particular topic, organizing them into a sheet with the alphabet on it. This initial brainstorm allows you to see what terms a student already knows about a topic, assessing background knowledge. Over the course of a unit, the student can add to the alphabet sheet as appropriate. To use this strategy as post-assessment, at the end of a unit, present students with a blank alphabet sheet, and ask them to fill in as many terms as they can remember about the topic of study. You can easily quantify the number of terms students knew at the beginning of the unit and compare it to the number of terms they knew at the end of the unit.

Allen (2010) created a version of this strategy, called Wordstorming. In this strategy, the teacher gives students the title of a text they are about to read or a brief description of content to be covered and a blank ABC template.

The teacher then gives only three sets of letters around which students are to brainstorm words; Allen reasons that for students with limited or no background to brainstorm around, presenting them with the entire alphabet immediately puts them at a deficit. By limiting the letters to ones that easily relate to the subject, students have a better chance of identifying a term or two for the sheet. Students share their brainstorms. This again allows the instructor time to see what misconceptions students may have about a topic. The template concludes with the students making a prediction about the content of the lecture or text and creating three questions that the content should answer. A blank example of this template is on page 54.

Common Core Connection

The strategies presented above fit well with a variety of standards in the Common Core State Standards for English Language Arts and the Literacy Standards for History/Social Studies, Science, and Technical Subjects. They are presented by grade level and content area in Figure 4.15.

Figure 4.15 Common Core State Standards

Grade Level	4	5	6
Standard Addressed	**Reading Standard for Informational Text** Determine the meaning of general academic and domain-specific words and phrases in a text relevant to a *grade 4 topic or subject area*. **Language Standard** Determine or clarify the meaning of unknown and multi-ple-meaning words and phrases based on *grade 4 reading and content*, choosing flexibly from a range of strategies.	**Reading Standard for Informational Text** Determine the meaning of general academic and domain-specific words and phrases in a text relevant to a *grade 5 topic or subject area*. **Language Standard** Determine or clarify the meaning of unknown and multi-ple-meaning words and phrases based on *grade 5 reading and content*, choosing flexibly from a range of strategies.	**Reading Standard for Informational Text** Determine the meaning of words and phrases as they are used in a text, including figurative, connotative, and technical meanings. **Language Standard** Determine or clarify the meaning of unknown and multi-ple-meaning words and phrases based on *grade 6 reading and content*, choosing flexibly from a range of strategies.

Grade Level	7	8	9–10
Standard Addressed	**Reading Standard for Informational Text** Determine the meaning of words and phrases as they are used in a text, including figurative, connotative, and technical meanings; analyze the impact of a specific word choice on meaning and tone. **Language Standard** Determine or clarify the meaning of unknown and multiple-meaning words and phrases based on *grade 7 reading and content*, choosing flexibly from a range of strategies.	**Reading Standard for Informational Text** Determine the meaning of words and phrases as they are used in a text, including figurative, connotative, and technical meanings. **Language Standard** Determine or clarify the meaning of unknown and multiple-meaning words or phrases based on *grade 8 reading and content*, choosing flexibly from a range of strategies. **Language Standard** Use the relationship between particular words to better understand each of the words.	**Reading Standard for Informational Text** Determine the meaning of words and phrases as they are used in a text, including figurative, connotative, and technical meanings; analyze the cumulative impact of specific word choices on meaning and tone (e.g., how the language of a court opinion differs from that of a newspaper).

Content Area	Social Studies	Science
Standard Addressed	Determine the meaning of words and phrases as they are used in a text, including vocabulary specific to domains related to history/social studies.	Determine the meaning of symbols, key terms, and other domain-specific words and phrases as they are used in a specific scientific or technical context relevant to *grades 6–8 texts and topics*. Analyze the structure of the relationships among concepts in a text, including relationships among key terms (e.g., *force, friction, reaction force, energy*).

Source: NGAC/CCSSO, 2010

Action Steps

There are many ways to assess a student's knowledge of key terms across content areas! Take some action:

1. When you have a unit of study coming up, decide what the end goal is in getting students to learn the unit's key terms and what the essential understanding is you want them to walk away with in terms of vocabulary acquisition in this unit (Wiggins & McTighe, 2005). Write that here:

    _____

    _____

    _____

    _____

    _____

2. Now that you see your goal, decide how you are going to check, both formatively and summatively, to see whether students are accomplishing it. Write how many of each type of assessment you plan on using:

    Formative assessments: _____

    _____

    Summative assessment: _____

    _____

3. Be specific. Which assessments were you drawn to the most? Which do you think will help you check student progress in accomplishing your goal from #1? List the assessments you plan on using here:

    Formative assessment #1: _____

    _____

    Formative assessment #2: _____

    _____

    Formative assessment #3: _____

    _____

    Summative assessment #1: _____

    _____

4. Challenge: Which of the assessments you listed can be both a pre- and a post-assessment? Pick one and use it at both the beginning and the end of the unit. How did the assessment show growth?

_____

_____

_____

_____

_____

5. REFLECT: Which assessment gave you the best picture of student mastery of the key terms of the unit? Why? Which formative assessment helped you see where students were in their acquisition of the vocabulary?

_____

_____

_____

_____

_____

Think-Pair-Share

Question or Prompt	What I thought	What my partner thought	What we will share

My Name: _____ Partner's Name: _____ Date: _____

Wordstorming to Anticipate Content

A–B	C–D	E–F	G–H

I–J	K–L	M–N	O–P

Q–R	S–T	U–V	W–X–Y–Z

Content Prediction:

Questions Article Should Answer:

Chapter 5

Teach Students Morphological Strategies to Figure Out Words They Do Not Know, in Addition to Context-Clue Strategies

Sarah threw down her book in anger during our conference. "I just don't know what this word means!" she exclaimed, after my repeated prompting to use context clues to figure out the meaning. "I read the sentence over and over again to myself, but the meaning doesn't magically come to me. The sentence just doesn't help. What else can I do besides skipping it?" She looked up at me with pleading eyes. "It seems like an important word, and it is hard for me to move on when I know I don't know what it means."

Why This Item Is Important

Sarah's frustration played out over the course of the year during our Readers Workshop conferencing. She was an inquisitive, bright girl who wanted to know everything, and not knowing the meaning of a word on a page annoyed her to no end. We had talked as a class about context clues as a means for figuring out these words, but Sarah was right; there were definitely sentences when going back and rereading the sentence did not help. Allen (2010) points out the reason for this: Local context (the rest of the sentence containing the unknown word) is reliable in only about 1 in 20 sentences when trying to figure out an unknown word. Science textbooks are brilliant in doing this; they often set apart the definitions of important vocabulary using commas within the sentence, clearly signaling to the reader "here's the definition!" In most fiction, however, the reader often needs more than just localized context clues to figure out an unknown word. They might need to go back and reread an entire paragraph (something many of our struggling readers are reluctant to do), or they need to continue reading in hopes that the word is explained further on (something readers like Sarah refused to do).

Arming students with strategies to figure out unknown words independently is imperative. Direct instruction on vocabulary terms by an expert teacher yields a student about 350 new vocabulary words in an academic year; however, students need to learn between 3,000 and 5,000 new words every year to move a grade level in terms of reading progression (Baumann, Edwards, Boland, Olejnik, & Kame'enui, 2003). Helping students recognize which strategy to use to figure out these words helps students reach the critical mass of words needed to be an expert reader.

> **Do This–Not That** principle #5: **DO** help students learn to use strategies to figure out the meanings of unknown words independently; **DON'T** prompt students to use only context clues.

To Get Started

Morphology, the study of Greek and Latin roots, and the use of context clues should not be an either-or situation when it comes to vocabulary instruction. A powerful quote emphasizes this point:

> For every word a child learns, we estimate that there are an average of one to three additional related words that should also be understandable to the child, the exact number depending on how well the child is able to use context and morphology to induce meanings. (Nagy & Anderson, 1984)

Both strategies provide students with strategies to figure out unknown words. When updating instructional practices, be sensitive to the fact that one cannot be sacrificed at the expense of another. However, the content area that tackles each word attack strategy is up for debate. As stated before, science textbooks are often the right place to show how authors utilize context clues to help readers. All content areas have important words that reflect Greek and Latin roots. A common complaint I hear from schools that are moving toward a systematic approach to teaching either system is that the burden falls to the language arts teacher, who often feels that teaching these skills in isolation leads to little application by students. The ideal scenario is twofold:

1. One teacher (generally, the language arts teacher) supplies the initial instruction in the different types of context clues and a variety of root words over the course of the year. Students are provided time in this class to apply this new knowledge to their self-selected and guided texts.

2. Other content teachers use "teachable moments" to highlight the occurrence and need for these strategies within their own texts. For example, if the root *tri* was introduced during word study in language arts, this would be a perfect time for the math teacher to show students the application of the root in math while talking about the different types of triangles.

Of course, to make this scenario work, teachers across content areas must carefully plan and have explicit dialogue. It behooves a team of teachers working with the same group of students to sit down and pace the list of Greek and Latin roots to be taught in language arts in such a way that they are mirrored in another content area (math, science, social studies, and specials) so that students get an immediate cross-curricular connection.

Updated Strategy #1: Teaching Each Type of Context Clue Specifically

Beers (2002) is very clear on context clues with struggling readers; she explains that teachers must first show students the different types of context clues and then give readers time to identify and use these different types to figure out unknown words. Many teachers give the directive I gave Sarah in the introduction "Use the context!" but for a struggling reader, this directive is even more of a mystery than the unknown word. Some teachers go on to explain at least what the word *context* means, and for good readers, this might be enough. For dependent readers, teachers need to go further.

Experts disagree on the number of types of context clues—a search yielded between four and six types. Here are the four basic types:

1. **Synonym:** A word with the same meaning is used within the same sentence.
   Example: The morning's rainstorm dissipated when the clouds separated and disappeared to the north and south.

2. **Antonym:** A word or group of words that has the opposite meaning reveals the meaning of an unknown word.
   Example: She thought her husband would like her new haircut, but he loathed it.

3. **Explanation:** The unknown word is explained within the sentence or in a sentence immediately preceding or following.

Example: The geologist, a person who studies rocks and minerals, bent low over the ground with his magnifying glass, eager to get a closer look at the specimen.

4. **Example:** Specific examples are used within the sentence to help define the unknown word.
   Example: Constellations, such as the Big Dipper and Orion, can be seen in the night sky.

The following instructional routine supports the instruction and practice of the four basic types of context clues across content areas:

♦ A teacher (usually the language arts teacher) introduces students to modeling one type of context clue. Several examples are shown of how authors employ this type of context clue in their writing. Think alouds are important here. When students come to a word they don't know, they often do not have a process in place for working through an unknown word. If a teacher models his or her thinking while applying the knowledge of the context clue to the word, it helps frame the process for struggling readers.

♦ Through guided practice, students work with a partner or small group to find this type of context clue in select class texts. Using worksheets or isolated text does not support students in grasping how to apply this new knowledge.

♦ Students are prompted to use a specific type of context clue when figuring out unknown words in self-selected reading. Beers (2002) strongly emphasizes this point; rather than saying, "Use your context clues," the teacher prompts, "That looks like the example type of context clue. Can you see how the author uses this to help you figure out that word?" A template that students can use to record unknown words in their self-selected reading and then the context clue or strategy they used to figure it out is included at the end of this chapter.

♦ Students are prompted to use context clues in their own writing. For example, if students have just learned about the synonym type of context clue, the next writing mini-lesson could be how and why to work this into an informative writing piece. This takes the skill from simply identifying context clues to applying the new knowledge.

♦ To support the instruction of the primary teacher, other teachers identify examples of the explicit context clue in the texts they will be using. Students can be prompted to use the context clue, *and* teachers can model using the context clue to think aloud through the meaning of the word across content areas.

A point that will be underscored repeatedly in this chapter is time for content area teachers to talk while planning instruction around these topics. In the case of context clues, the planning is simple; the primary teacher responsible for the initial instruction informs his or her teaching partners that during this particular week or period, they will be covering this type of context clue. It is then up to the rest of the team members to touch upon it in their own teaching, knowing that if they do it well, students will be more likely to understand and apply the concept.

Updated Strategy #2: Teaching Students Greek and Latin Words to Figure Out Unknown Words

If you need a few reasons to consider implementing the teaching of Greek and Latin roots in your classroom, consider these points:

- 60% of multisyllabic words in the English language are derived from Greek and Latin (Bromley, 2007).

- A single Greek or Latin root can help students understand 20 or more English words (Rasinski, Padak, Newton, & Newton, 2010).

- Because Spanish is a derivative of Greek and Latin, the study of their roots in the English language may be helpful to English language learners whose native language is Spanish or other romance languages such as French and Italian (Rasinski et al., 2010).

- In the Common Core State Standards, Greek and Latin roots appear as early as grade one, where students are asked to "use frequently occurring affixes as a clue to the meaning of a word" (NGAC/CCSSO, 2010).

Now that the "why" of teaching Greek and Latin roots is out of the way, let's address the "how" through a series of questions:

- How do I decide which Greek and Latin root words to teach?

Different schools approach this question in three ways:

1. Prepackaged programs exist that provide weekly lessons on one or two roots per week, along with strategies and assessments to create an instructional routine. Some are even leveled so that grade levels can build on a previous year's knowledge as students acquire new word parts. While these provide ease in planning, they can be disconnected from the students' learning in other areas (for example, the student is studying Greek and Latin body parts in language arts but is not applying the knowledge of these roots anywhere else in the curriculum). I would urge schools that take this route to work to ensure that the roots being studied as part of the program are highlighted and enhanced in other curricular areas.

2. Other schools pace a list of root words among grade levels. Foundational root word knowledge is presented in lower grades and built upon in successive grades. These lists can often be more responsive to curricular needs; time will end up being the most precious commodity as many different voices from content areas need to be represented in order to select and structure these word lists to reflect a variety of content areas at appropriate times throughout the year. A starting place with this approach should be a list of common Greek and Latin root words; this gives teachers a basis to begin the search through their own curricula for appropriate words to add to the school or grade level list (a sample list for your own use is on page 69).

3. A final approach is more content isolated; teachers look at their own curricula to select and highlight Tier 2 or 3 words that contain Greek and Latin roots and plan to teach these words and word parts when they appear throughout the year. The key to this approach is having a common word study routine with these words so that students can spend their brainpower learning and applying their new word knowledge and not learning a new word routine with each content area teacher (suggestions for such a routine with word parts follows).

Whichever approach you or your school or school system takes, it is important to be consistent. Any program must be implemented with fidelity; lists developed by grade levels across content areas must be followed, and a more holistic approach, like the one described in 3, should be shared and discussed across grade levels.

♦ How do I establish a routine for studying Greek and Latin roots in my classroom?

Several of the word study strategies presented in this text can be used to study words with Greek and Latin roots: Concept Maps, Alike but Different, and Vocabulary Reader's Theater (Chapter 3) can all be used to help students explore and take ownership of words with Greek and Latin roots. What follows in this section are three instructional strategies that work particularly well when studying a specific root:

1. **The Root Word Tree** (Bromley, 2007): The root word tree is a strategy that helps students do exactly what Nagy and Anderson were addressing in their quote earlier in this chapter—if students know a word (or a word part, in this case) they are able to use this transactional knowledge to learn about other words. The sample shown in Figure 5.1 came from a seventh-grade science teacher. All the seventh-grade teachers had come together to create a list of words that crossed content areas. They

paced the words so that different content areas were responsible for teaching the roots that were featured in their content throughout the year. In a unit about astronomy, the word *telescope* was featured. The science teacher presented the root word *tele* to his seventh graders. With a partner, they brainstormed as many different words as they could think of that contained the root *tele*. He passed out the Root Tree graphic organizer (Figure 5.1) to his students so they could fill it in (a blank template is on page 70).

After students filled in the graphic organizer, they used their sample words to come up with a meaning for the root *tele*.

One grade level that was working on Greek and Latin roots decided to take the idea of root word trees to the next level; they created butcher-paper trees in the hallways between their classrooms and let each branch represent a different root they were studying. During the week,

Figure 5.1   Sample Root Tree Graphic Organizer

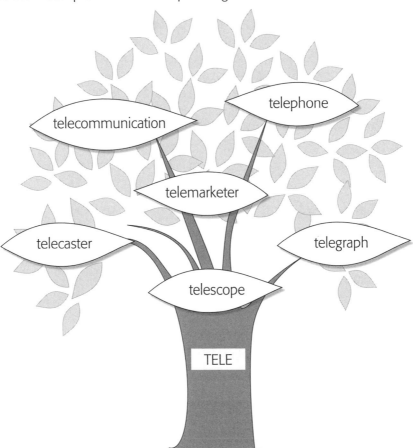

as students came across or brainstormed words that contained this root, they wrote the word on a leaf that contained the root. The trees "bloomed" across the hallways, a constant visual reminder of the interconnectedness of Greek and Latin roots!

It goes without saying that there are some roots that are easier to generate a variety of words with. A great resource for lists of words using different root words is www.morewords.com. In the search engine on the home page, simply type in "words containing _____," and it will generate every word with that spelling combination. Word of caution: the spelling combination is not always the root, so be sure to read the list carefully for outliers!

2. **Word Sorts** (Fisher et al., 2011; Fisher & Frey, 2011): Word sorts are a great way to introduce, reinforce, and assess students' knowledge of Greek and Latin roots. In creating their word study routine, the teachers of Maple Heights City Schools use word sorts twice. When a new root is being introduced, students are handed an envelope. In the envelope is the root in a variety of words on individual slips of paper. Individually or with a partner, students are asked to sort the words in a way that makes sense to them, often before they are told what the root means. A sample of word study slips using the root *arch* in seventh-grade social studies is shown in Figure 5.2.

Figure 5.2   Word Sort with Root *arch*

archangel	monarch	myriarch
archenemy	anarchy	biarchy

Many students see the six words shown in Figure 5.2 and put the words that have *arch* in the beginning in one column and the other three in another column. Others might sort them into words they know (in this particular class, many students knew *monarch* and *archangel*) and words they are not familiar with. No answer is right or wrong in an initial sort; instead, students must be able to provide a rationale for why they sorted them that way *based on the root*. This is italicized for a reason; sorting just for the sake of sorting (alphabetical, shortest to longest) does not help students in learning about a new root word!

Later in the week, after students have been introduced to the meaning of the root word and have had experience brainstorming other words with the root (with the Root Tree!), the word sort envelopes come out again. This time, the sorting is more purposeful and quick, allowing the students to demonstrate that they have learned the meaning of the root.

3. **Wordo** (Fisher et al, 2011): Wordo (think bingo) is a fun game that allows students to apply their knowledge of a single root to multiple words. Students receive a game card with derivatives of a single root on it. I highly recommend having the game cards already made up for the students instead of giving them a blank grid to fill out (the result is often more time spent filling in the game card or cheating than actually playing the game!). Teachnology (www.teach-nology.com/web_tools/ materials/bingo/) has a great, free bingo card generator that allows you to input the words of your choice into a template and create multiple cards at the push of a button. Figure 5.3 shows a sample of a card using the root *port*.

Figure 5.3 Sample Wordo Card

Airport	Comport	Deport
Export	Import	Important
Misreported	Opportunist	Passport

To play Wordo, the teacher (or a student, once the class gets comfortable with the definitions) calls out a certain type of bingo game, such as four corners, diagonal, vertical, or horizontal line. He or she then calls out the different definitions of *port* words, pausing to allow students to mark off the words on their cards. When a student reaches the designated shape, he or she calls out *Wordo*! This simple review game is a fun way for students to show definitional knowledge of their Greek and Latin root words.

Common Core Connection

The strategies just presented fit well with a variety of standards in the Common Core State Standards. They are presented by grade level and content area in Figure 5.4.

Figure 5.4 Common Core State Standards for English Language Arts and Literacy Standards for History/Social Studies, and Technical Subjects

Grade Level	4	5	6
Standard Addressed	**Language Standard** Determine or clarify the meaning of unknown and multiple-meaning words and phrases based on *grade 4 reading and content,* choosing flexibly from a range of strategies. a. Use context (e.g., definitions, examples, or restatements in text) as a clue to the meaning of a word or phrase. b. Use common, grade-appropriate Greek and Latin affixes and roots as clues to the meaning of a word (e.g., *telegraph, photograph, autograph*). ... c. Demonstrate understanding of words by relating them to their opposites (antonyms) and to words with similar but not identical meanings (synonyms).	**Language Standard** Determine or clarify the meaning of unknown and multiple-meaning words and phrases based on *grade 5 reading and content,* choosing flexibly from a range of strategies. a. Use context (e.g., cause/effect relationships and comparisons in text) as a clue to the meaning of a word or phrase. b. Use common, grade-appropriate Greek and Latin affixes and roots as clues to the meaning of a word (e.g., *photograph, photosynthesis*). c. Use the relationship between particular words (e.g., synonyms, antonyms, homographs) to better understand each of the words.	**Language Standard** a. Use context (e.g., the overall meaning of a sentence or paragraph; a word's position or function in a sentence) as a clue to the meaning of a word or phrase. b. Use common, grade-appropriate Greek or Latin affixes and roots as clues to the meaning of a word (e.g., *audience, auditory, audible*).

Grade Level	7	8	9–10
Standard Addressed	**Language Standard** Determine or clarify the meaning of unknown and multiple-meaning words and phrases based on *grade 7 reading and content*, choosing flexibly from a range of strategies. a. Use context (e.g., the overall meaning of a sentence or paragraph; a word's position or function in a sentence) as a clue to the meaning of a word or phrase. b. Use common, grade-appropriate Greek or Latin affixes and roots as clues to the meaning of a word (e.g., *belligerent, bellicose, rebel*).	**Language Standard** Determine or clarify the meaning of unknown and multiple-meaning words or phrases based on *grade 8 reading and content*, choosing flexibly from a range of strategies. a. Use context (e.g., the overall meaning of a sentence or paragraph; a word's position or function in a sentence) as a clue to the meaning of a word or phrase. b. Use common, grade-appropriate Greek or Latin affixes and roots as clues to the meaning of a word (e.g., *precede, recede, secede*).	**Language Standard** Determine or clarify the meaning of unknown and multiple-meaning words and phrases based on *grades 9–10 reading and content*, choosing flexibly from a range of strategies. a. Use context (e.g., the overall meaning of a sentence, paragraph, or text; a word's position or function in a sentence) as a clue to the meaning of a word or phrase. b. Identify and correctly use patterns of word changes that indicate different meanings or parts of speech (e.g., *analyze, analytical; advocate, advocacy*).

Action Steps

The teaching of specific context clues and Greek and Latin roots enhances students' knowledge of vocabulary across content areas. Take some action:

1. Tackling both the teaching of context clue types and Greek and Latin root words at the same time can be overwhelming. Either with your teaching team or individually, decide which word attack strategy you will introduce first. Why did you choose this strategy?

_____

_____

_____

_____

2. If you chose context clues, you have a few ideas to consider:

   a. In what order will you teach students the context clue types?

     _____

     _____

     _____

   b. What texts will you use to have students do guided practice in finding and using the different context clue types?

     _____

     _____

     _____

   c. How will you formatively assess student use of the different types of context clues?

     _____

     _____

     _____

   d. If you teach on a team, how will you communicate and support your colleagues in providing supplementary teaching in the different context clues?

     _____

     _____

     _____

3. If you chose Greek and Latin roots, you have ideas to consider, too.

   a. Which type of implementation will you use? A prepackaged program, team approach, or individual content area approach with a common word study routine? Why did you choose that route?

     _____

     _____

     _____

   b. How will you sequence words for maximum impact?

     _____

     _____

     _____

c. Which word study strategy(s) will you use? Why?

_____

_____

_____

4. REFLECT: How did the implementation of word attack strategies go? Are students better able to use either morphology or context clues to figure out unknown words?

_____

_____

_____

_____

_____

Record Sheet for Context Clues

Word & page number	Type of context clue	Definition

Common Greek and Latin Roots

Elementary Level Latin and Greek Roots and Affixes

Prefixes	Definition
a-, ab-, abs-	away, from
ad-	to, toward, add to
co-, com-, con-, col-	with, together
de-	own, off of
di-, dif-, dis-	apart, in different directions, not
ex-	out
in-, im-, il-	in, on, into (*directional*)
in-, im-, il-	not (*negative*)
pre-	before
pro-	forward, ahead
re-	back, again
sub-	under, below
tra-, tran-, tans	across, change
un-	not (*negative*)

Parallel Latin and Greek Prefixes		Definition
Latin	**Greek**	
contra-, contro-, counter-	anti-	against
circu-, circum-	peri-	around
multi-	poly-	many
super-, sur-	hyper-	over
sub-	hypo-	under, below

Bases	Definition
audi-, audit-	hear, listen
cred-, credit-	believe
cur-, curs-, cours-	run, go
dict-	say, tell, speak
duc-, duct-	lead
fac-, fic-, fact-, fect-	do, make
graph-, gram-	write, draw
mis-, mit-	send
mov-, mot-, mobil-	move
pon-, pos-, posit-	put, place
port-	carry
scrib-	script, write
terr-	earth
vid-, vis-	see

Numerical Bases (appear at beginning of words)	Definition
uni-	one
bi-	two
tri-	three

Parallel Latin and Greek Bases		Definition
Latin	**Greek**	
aqua-	hydro-	water
ped-	pod-	foot, feet
terr-	geo-	earth

Source: Rasinski et al., 2010

Root Word Tree Template

Chapter 6

Use Symbols and Pictures to Help Bring Vocabulary to Life

I noticed in my first classroom that the students, when given an opportunity to use a dictionary, gravitated toward the dictionaries that had pictures. These dictionaries were meant for a much younger audience, but my English language learners fought over them. I assumed it was because the definitions were easier to figure out but Maria, who was sulking over a regular dictionary, finally explained it to me: "The pictures, Miss, bring the words to life. I might not know how to read all the words yet, but the pictures help me understand and remember what the word means."

Why This Item Is Important

Maria perfectly elaborated why symbols and pictures are vital to use when teaching vocabulary. Klinger, Vaughn, and Boardman (2007) define visualization as a skill that allows students to represent new knowledge, retrieve previously learned knowledge, organize and store information, draw conclusions, and explain comprehension by turning visualizations back into words. When I ask you what you did last weekend, a typewriter doesn't flash a message across your brain with a description of you lying on the couch, watching TV, and eating a good meal. Instead, pictures come to your mind of you lolling on the couch, remote in hand, or you visualize your spot at the dinner table with the spread in front of you. We remember our lives in pictures; it makes sense to help students remember new word meanings in the same way.

> **Do This–Not That** principle #6: **DO** allow students to include pictures and symbols in their acquisition of new vocabulary; **DON'T** limit students to plain text only!

To Get Started

Marzano (2010) describes the use of pictures and symbols to learn information as "nonlinguistic representation of text." His research shows that use of techniques that capitalize on nonlinguistic representation of text can increase student achievement by as much as seventeen percent (Marzano, 2010). Marzano provides five keys to making nonlinguistic representations of text work:

1. *Nonlinguistic representations of text can come in many forms.* There isn't one "right way" to help a student use this strategy when many different types of symbols, pictures, pictographs, graphic organizers, and charts can help words make sense.

2. *Nonlinguistic representations of text must represent crucial information.* In his study, Marzano found that this strategy is useful only when students use nonlinguistic representations of text to show the most important information to be learned.

3. *Students should explain their nonlinguistic representations.* Simply drawing is not enough. Students need to explain the thought process behind the symbolism, allowing them to exert metacognition in their learning and alerting the teacher to any misconceptions.

4. *Nonlinguistic representations can take a lot of time.* This is why Marzano emphasizes using them only to present important information.

5. *Students should revise their representations when necessary.* As students' knowledge evolves, so should their initial drawings. If they learn new information on a topic they have already drawn, they should have the time to amend any nonlinguistic representations to show their new knowledge.

Continuing through this book and examining new strategies to update your instructional practice, keep in mind the strategies presented previously that build on this premise:

- Alike but Different (Chapter 2): At the bottom of the graphic organizer, under "How I'll Remember," students draw pictures to help them remember the meanings of the words being compared.

- Concept Maps (Chapter 2): Instead of having students give nonexamples of the word being studied, have them draw the meaning of the word.

- PowerPoint (Chapter 3): Display important vocabulary for the day along with a picture that illustrates the meaning.

Updated Strategy #1: Using Sketch to Stretch

The original intent of Sketch to Stretch was to allow students to visualize what they were reading. Students read a short passage in a longer text or story (or listen while a text is read aloud to them) and then are given a short amount of time to draw their reaction to the story or what they think just happened. When students have finished reading or listening to the story, they have created a series of drawings to help them remember the text (McLaughlin & Allen, 2002; Rasinski & Padak, 2000).

Sketch to Stretch accomplishes many things for the reader:

- It chunks the text so that students are concentrating on one short passage at a time rather than trying to digest an entire text.

- It forces students to stop and think about the text periodically, ensuring that meaning-making is happening throughout reading.

- It allows students to apply the theory of nonlinguistic representation of text in a fun, natural way.

To bring this strategy to vocabulary study, invite students to read a short passage in a longer text or story. At the conclusion of the passage, ask students to select one word to examine closely. This word should be pertinent to the meaning of the passage; modeling which word to choose and why it is vital! Students then draw what they think the word means in the passage. Students continue on, stopping periodically to select and sketch important words in the text. These words can then be added to a class word wall, nominated for study in Vocabulary Self-Selection, or simply discussed with a partner as to which words were selected and why. To teach this strategy to students, use the following gradual release of responsibility steps:

1. **Modeling:** Present a shared text to students. Designate a few paragraphs to use for the first instance of Sketch to Stretch. After reading the first section, present to students statements that can be used to help determine if a word is worthy of investigation (Figure 6.1). Once a word is selected using these statements, model for students how you puzzle through your sketch of this word. Emphasize that students have only two to three minutes to do their sketch; no Picassos expected!

2. **Nominating:** Read through the next section of text with students. Stop and allow students to nominate a word for study, using the statements in Figure 6.1 to qualify their choices. Select a word, and invite students to sketch the meaning of the word in context for two to three minutes. Allow students to share their drawings with their neighbors, comparing their different approaches to the word.

3. **Stopping to sketch:** Ask students to finish reading the passage. Remind students to stop periodically throughout the text to sketch the meaning of important words (designate a number, or set up the page so that students are visually reminded to stop reading and select a word to sketch—see Figure 6.2).

Figure 6.1   Is a Word Worthy of Investigation?

1. I won't understand the entire selection if I don't know what this word means.
2. I see that this word is used again later in the text.
3. The use of this word in context is different from the definition I usually remember with this word.
4. This word interests, puzzles, or delights me!

Figure 6.2   Sample Sketch to Stretch Passage and Template

Floors shook. Books toppled off shelves. Ceilings fell. The power went out. That's what happened in Chile recently. A powerful earthquake struck the South American nation. Hundreds of people were killed. Millions were left homeless. "It was the scariest experience of my life, just a violent shake. My thought was the house was going to come falling down," Sarah Botkin, 27, told a reporter in her home state of Washington. She teaches English in Santiago, Chile's capital city.	Word _____ Sketch: Meaning in context:
The news of what happened in Chile was all too familiar. The quake came not long after the Haiti earthquake. That disaster devastated the poor Caribbean nation. Officials now estimate that 230,000 people were killed. As people worldwide work to help the victims of these natural disasters, many are wondering why nature is acting up—and if it will continue to do so.	Word _____ Sketch: Meaning in context:
The earthquakes in Haiti and Chile occurred where earthquakes usually do—on the edges of huge plates on the Earth's surface. Called **tectonic** plates, these giant slabs of earth fit together like a puzzle (see map). As they move, the plates pull apart from, collide with, or slide against one another. Sometimes pressure builds up, causing pieces of the plates to break. This releases energy that can cause the ground to shake violently. Earthquakes are often followed by related quakes, called aftershocks.	Word _____ Sketch: Meaning in context:

Source: Excerpted from Scholastic News, 2010.

Limiting students to the number of bold or italicized words they can choose when selecting words to sketch can be helpful. A full template of the Sketch to Stretch vocabulary sheet is included on page 81.

Updated Strategy #2: Employing A–Z Charts

Useful in content areas, A–Z Charts can be used to help students collect important vocabulary on a topic for study (Fisher & Frey, 2008). To take this strategy a step further, students can collect important vocabulary around a topic alphabetically, and they can sketch the words they collect.

Part phonetic exercise, part graphic organizer, A–Z charts help students systematically organize their learning on a subject of study or even a chapter of a textbook. Excellent A–Z books (such as *D is for Democracy*, by Elissa Grodin) are models of how students can study a topic alphabetically as well as include pictures or sketches to promote learning and review of important terms. As with any long-term project, decide how polished you want these finished products to be. Are sketches enough? Can students use clip art or pictures from magazines? Most teachers simply want to encourage students to notice the important terms presented in the text, so having students list the terms under the appropriate letter, with an informal sketch, suffices for that purpose. Other teachers have students collaborate to create elaborate A–Z books on a variety of topics that become part of the class library or are used for later instruction. In any case, it is helpful to get students started by passing out the basic template (see page 82) and modeling expectations for students in completing the sheet (for example, depending on the topic, you might not fill in all spaces). Remind students periodically to take out their A–Z sheets and to add to them so that by the time an assessment rolls around, the review sheet is waiting for them! An example of a few letters for an A–Z chart on sixth-grade geometry is shown in Figure 6.3.

Figure 6.3 A–Z Chart Example

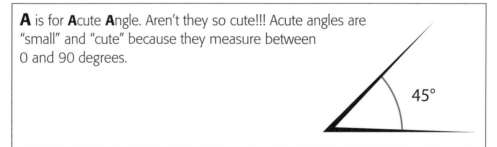

A is for **A**cute **A**ngle. Aren't they so cute!!! Acute angles are "small" and "cute" because they measure between 0 and 90 degrees.

45°

B is for **B**ase. No, not a base in baseball! A base in geometry is the bottom of a shape (such as a triangle) and sometimes the top, too (such as a trapezoid).

C is for **C**ircumference. Since tape measures don't bend really well, circumference helps measure the distance around a circle! Using the formula C = 2πr where r is the radius makes it easy!

Updated Strategy #3: Using Three-Dimensional Words

Bromley (2007) combined several models of vocabulary study to create a word study strategy called Three-Dimensional Words. In this strategy, students are required to define a word, use it in context, draw a representation of the word, *and* find a real-life object to help the students learn the definition. This strategy is deceptively simple, but many words do not lend themselves well to the real-life object! The key is to get creative; Bromley gives an example of the word *identical*. The definition, sentence, and drawing are to be expected; the real-life objects are two paper clips taped to the page.

To scaffold this strategy, model with the template explicitly (see page 84). Like the Frayer Model, this strategy should be done with only a word or two, not an entire list. Bromley (2007) suggests allowing a group of students to create a page for a word and then allowing groups to meet with other groups to use their page to teach about their word. These can then be displayed around the room to allow students to use these three-dimensional definitions of words of study as reminders.

Common Core Connection

Of course, symbols and pictures are not directly mentioned in the Common Core State Standards; however, these three strategies will assist students in mastering the standards shown in Figure 6.4.

Figure 6.4 Common Core State Standards

Grade Level	4	5	6
Standard Addressed	**Reading Standard for Informational Text** Determine the meaning of general academic and domain-specific words and phrases in a text relevant to a *grade 4 topic or subject area.* **Language Standard** Determine or clarify the meaning of unknown and multiple-meaning words and phrases based on *grade 4 reading and content*, choosing flexibly from a range of strategies.	**Reading Standard for Informational Text** Determine the meaning of general academic and domain-specific words and phrases in a text relevant to a *grade 5 topic or subject area.* **Language Standard** Determine or clarify the meaning of unknown and multiple-meaning words and phrases based on *grade 5 reading and content*, choosing flexibly from a range of strategies.	**Reading Standard for Informational Text** Determine the meaning of words and phrases as they are used in a text, including figurative, connotative, and technical meanings. **Language Standard** Determine or clarify the meaning of unknown and multiple-meaning words and phrases based on *grade 6 reading and content*, choosing flexibly from a range of strategies.

Grade Level	7	8	9–10
Standard Addressed	**Reading Standard for Informational Text** Determine the meaning of words and phrases as they are used in a text, including figurative, connotative, and technical meanings; analyze the impact of a specific word choice on meaning and tone. **Language Standard** Determine or clarify the meaning of unknown and multiple-meaning words and phrases based on *grade 7 reading and content*, choosing flexibly from a range of strategies.	**Reading Standard for Informational Text** Determine the meaning of words and phrases as they are used in a text, including figurative, connotative, and technical meanings; **Language Standard** Determine or clarify the meaning of unknown and multiple-meaning words or phrases based on *grade 8 reading and content*, choosing flexibly from a range of strategies.	**Reading Standard for Informational Text** Determine the meaning of words and phrases as they are used in a text, including figurative, connotative, and technical meanings; analyze the cumulative impact of specific word choices on meaning and tone (e.g., how the language of a court opinion differs from that of a newspaper).

Content Area	Social Studies	Science
Standard Addressed	Determine the meaning of words and phrases as they are used in a text, including vocabulary specific to domains related to history/social studies.	Determine the meaning of symbols, key terms, and other domain-specific words and phrases as they are used in a specific scientific or technical context relevant to grades 6–8 texts and topics.

Source: NGAC/CCSSO, 2010

Action Steps

Using pictures, symbols, charts, and real-life objects really helps words come alive for students! Take some action:

1. Try out the weekend activity with your students—ask them what they did last weekend. After soliciting a few answers, ask students if they saw words of what they did over the weekend or if they saw snapshots of the activities they participated in. Explain to students that this is simply how the human brain works; people remember information in pictures not words. Tell students that this exercise will help them as they try out new strategies to help them remember the meanings of important words. Write some notes on how it went.

   _____

   _____

   _____

2. Select one of the strategies to try out with your students from Sketch to Stretch, A–Z Charts, and Three-Dimensional Words.

   a. Which one did you choose? Why?

   _____

   _____

   _____

   b. Design a lesson sequence for this strategy. How will you model and guide practice in this strategy?

   _____

   _____

   _____

   c. How will you assess success in this strategy?

   _____

   _____

   _____

   d. REFLECT: Which strategy did you teach? Was it successful? Did it help students learn the word meanings? How do you know?

   _____

   _____

   _____

Sketch to Stretch

Word _____

Sketch:

Meaning in context:

Word _____

Sketch:

Meaning in context:

Word _____

Sketch:

Meaning in context:

Word _____

Sketch:

Meaning in context:

Word _____

Sketch:

Meaning in context:

Word _____

Sketch:

Meaning in context:

Word _____

Sketch:

Meaning in context:

Word _____

Sketch:

Meaning in context:

Word _____

Sketch:

Meaning in context:

Word _____

Sketch:

Meaning in context:

Vocabulary ABCs

Topic _____

A _____

_____

_____

_____

B _____

_____

_____

_____

C _____

_____

_____

_____

D _____

_____

_____

_____

E _____

_____

_____

_____

F _____

_____

_____

_____

G _____

_____

_____

_____

H _____

_____

_____

_____

I _____

_____

_____

_____

J _____

_____

_____

_____

K _____

_____

_____

_____

L _____

_____

_____

_____

M _____

_____

_____

_____

N _____

_____

_____

_____

O _____

_____

_____

_____

P _____

_____

_____

_____

Q _____

_____

_____

_____

R _____

_____

_____

_____

S _____

_____

_____

_____

T _____

_____

_____

_____

U _____

_____

_____

_____

V _____

_____

_____

_____

W _____

_____

_____

_____

X _____

_____

_____

_____

Y _____

_____

_____

_____

Z _____

_____

_____

_____

Three-Dimensional Words

Word: _____

Definition (3 words or fewer!):

_____

_____

_____

Sketch:

Sentence using word:

_____

_____

_____

Real-life object:

Adapted from Bromley (2007)

Chapter 7

Highlight and Use a Word Wall in Classroom Instruction

In my first position as a literacy specialist in a large school district, one of the first moves I made was to purchase and distribute ready-made word walls to the teachers in grades K–6. Appropriate, high-frequency words for each grade level were to be systematically displayed throughout the year, with instructional time for games and study of the words in classrooms. However, it became apparent in the first few weeks of school that few, if any, teachers had been able to sit down, read the manual that came with the packet of words, and learn to use it as it had been designed. All the words were immediately stapled up on the wall, and they were rarely, if ever, used in instruction. Teachers were politely following the district mandate to have a word wall; they were missing the instruction on how to effectively use one in their classrooms.

Why This Item Is Important

The term *word wall* often conjures up a picture of a paper train running around the perimeter of an elementary school classroom. Each car of the train is a different letter and periodically, the teacher will add to the word wall with a high-frequency sight word or an interesting word that came up during a shared reading experience. However, word walls are and should be an integral part of word study in both the middle and high school classroom, across content areas.

Interactive word walls have been shown to increase test scores (Jackson, Tripp, & Cox, 2011; Yates, Cuthrell, & Rose, 2011), foster independence in reading and writing (Fisher & Frey, 2008), and serve as a reminder of the spiral curriculum in many classrooms (Grimes, 2009). And with as little as a stack of note cards and a permanent marker, a teacher can start a word wall immediately.

> **Do This–Not That** principle #7: **DO** highlight and use a word wall effectively in your classroom; **DON'T** lack a word wall or have one and not use it to your students' benefit.

To Get Started

Let's start with a shared definition of a word wall: "a collection of developmentally appropriate vocabulary displayed somewhere in the classroom" (Yates, Cuthrell, & Rose, 2011). No trains in sight with that definition! From there, we get into the real depth of what a word wall can do. Depending on your goals, a word wall can do the following:

♦ Create a visual map for the teacher and the students: As words are added to the word wall, they not only add to the print-rich environment of the room (Harmon, Wood, Hedrick, Vintinner, & Willeford, 2009; Graves & Watts-Taffe, 2008) but also help show everyone in the classroom what has been discussed. This also sneaks in multiple exposures to important terms (as discussed in Chapter 2).

♦ Promote independence: A well-crafted word wall can assist students in their reading, writing, and speaking (Yates et al., 2011). Since most words on the word wall should be formally taught, students can use it to help remind themselves of a word previously learned while reading or to help them incorporate more sophisticated language while writing and speaking.

♦ Highlight student choice and engagement: The best word wall words come from your students. And because word walls become a prominent feature in most classrooms, students now have a direct say in how the classroom is decorated. Like the Vocabulary Self-Selection strategy in Chapter 1, this feature of a word wall helps bring everyone together to not only decide which words to study but also put those choices literally up on the wall.

Types of Word Walls

There are three main types of word walls:

1. High-frequency-words word walls: This type is the one described at the beginning of the chapter. As younger students learn to read new sight words, this word wall displays these words, showing them how many they have learned.

2. Frequently-misspelled-words word walls: These abound in English classes where a frustrated teacher has decided he or she has had enough of the same words being misspelled over and over again (for example, *their*, *they're*, and *there*). These word walls often come with the statement "If a word is on the word wall and appears misspelled in your paper, you will lose points!"

3. Subject-specific word walls: These appear most often in math, science, social studies, and special classes. They can be organized by unit or chapter, time (Reconstruction, for example), or concept (such as astronomy).

With the basics of word walls behind us, let's delve deeper into the Do This–Not That principle of word walls: you can have the most beautiful word wall up in your classroom, full of colors, definitions, and drawings, organized with purpose, and displayed prominently; however, if you do not use the word wall effectively on a continual basis, then the whole purpose behind it is lost. Here are several tips for keeping your word wall as interactive as possible:

♦ *Begin the year or unit by introducing the word wall concept to your class* (Vallejo, 2006). Taking a class period to let students help you begin your word wall, as well as telling them why you are building one, lets students know that this is something of importance. Vallejo, a secondary high school science teacher, takes a class period at the beginning of the year to let students help measure out the space and begin to choose and illustrate terms for the first unit of study.

♦ *Create a routine for word wall work.* Make it a point to include word wall activities into your weekly plans. This can be as simple as having students comb through their reading or writing to find interesting words to add to an adjective word wall in language arts (Bromley, 2003) or making time to incorporate a word wall strategy or two into your word study routine.

♦ *Add, add, and then add some more to your word wall.* It is easy to begin a word wall and then let it go after a unit (or even a week). Also designate a time to add new words to your word wall. Many teachers like to do so after reading so that students can nominate words for study that they feel are central to the topic being covered (Harmon, Wood & Kiser, 2009).

♦ *Place the word wall in a place where both you and the students can see it and refer to it.* A side wall that is visible to everyone in the classroom is often the best place for a word wall. This way, the instructor can work important terms into his or her teaching because they are being visually reminded by the word wall, and the students do not have to twist too far in their seats to use the word wall while reading and writing. Often, I see word walls in the back of the classroom, where truly only the teacher can see it.

♦ *When the unit is over, get ready to build a new wall (but move the old words somewhere else).* This tip was born out of my own frustration. I disliked removing the old words from a word wall that we had worked so hard on. I began to transfer the words to unused places in the classroom, retiring them to a resting spot, where they could still remind us of their importance. The best underutilized space in the classroom is under the whiteboard or chalkboard, followed by above or below windows and doors and, of course, the ceiling. I especially like posting old word wall words on the ceiling; I noticed students daydreaming with their heads flung back, and I figured that a few words on the ceiling might help them remember previously learned concepts by osmosis (but check with your school's fire codes before you post anything up there!).

Updated Strategy #1: Building an Effective Word Wall

Let's start at the beginning of the school year. Your walls are empty and just itching to be decorated with inspirational posters. But wait! Before you post the school rules, decide on a spot for your main word wall. Simply mark off your space and possibly title your word wall, so when students walk in, they can see you have dedicated this spot in the room to word study.

If you are so inclined, chalkboard trays, open rain gutters, or halved PVC pipe can create fantastic, mobile word walls. When I began using word walls, I typically stapled or stuck the words to the wall with sticky tack. These tactics were great for displaying the words, but I found that when I wanted to use the cards for games or strategies (like the ones presented in Updated Strategies #2 and #3 later in this chapter), I had to either make a second stack of note cards with the same words or pull the words off the wall and then stick them back up later. Frustrated, I began to place the cards across my chalkboard at the front of the classroom. Anytime I wanted to use my words, I simply had to run my hand down the chalk tray and pick them up. Inspired,

I went to my local hardware store and bought five three-foot lengths of open rain gutters and had them drilled into my wall on the side of my classroom. I set the cards in the rain gutters and could pick them up and use them whenever I wanted (this works well for displaying books, too!).

Once you have your spot, decide which type of word wall will suit your instructional purposes best. Jackson et al. (2011) note that merely posting words on the wall does little for learning; having a structure in mind (or an activity in which students help you create a structure) is helpful. Vallejo (2006) begins his word wall by distributing one or two words per student that he has predetermined as important for the first unit of study. He models how to write neatly and largely on the provided card and how to include a symbol or picture with the word to help students remember the definition (Chapter 6). Although the students are creating the cards in this scenario, the teacher chose the words. To create further buy-in, you can use the cards as a pre-test to see what students already know about the important terms in an upcoming unit. Spread the words out on the floor, and gather the class around so that students can see them. Ask students to make recommendations for organizing the words; essentially you are seeing what connections students can already make about the terms. As the unit progresses, students can revisit the organization of the words to match their new knowledge.

The next type of word-wall building is allowing students to choose the words to study. To ensure that the words fall into the necessary categories, you might provide labels under which students can submit words for the word wall. For example, for a unit on astronomy, you might have labels such as Basic Concepts, Models of Study, and Important Laws. Then, as students read and study, they can look for terms that can be added under those labels, ensuring an easy fit with your instruction.

To really let students take the lead in the creation of a word wall, List-Group-Label is an excellent strategy that gives students full control of words to be posted on a word wall while allowing you to see background knowledge on a topic (Tierney & Readence, 2000). This strategy is not new; in fact, the first reference to it is from 1967 (Taba, 1967)! In this strategy, give students a topic around which to brainstorm important terms, such as immigration in social studies. As a class, you and your students list all possible terms on the board. In pairs or small groups, students work together to logically group the words. Once students have grouped the words, they come up with labels for their groupings. An eighth-grade example of a List-Group-Label is shown in Figure 7.1 on page 90.

As you can see, these students worked recursively to both group and label the words. They found it easier to brainstorm labels and then see how many words they could fit into those groups. With your class, find out what

Figure 7.1 Eighth-Grade List-Group-Label on Immigration

Immigration
tenement   motto   persecution   ethnic group   refugee Ellis Island   Statue of Liberty
heritage   citizen   culture   immigrant   immigrate naturalization   boat   slave
papers   New York   Mexico   dangerous   scary   food   languages

Group & Label
Words that describe immigration: dangerous, scary
Places people immigrate from and to: Ellis Island, New York, Statue of Liberty, Mexico
Things immigrants brought to America: heritage, culture, food, languages, papers
Reasons people came to America: persecution, refugee, slave
Words that don't fit anywhere: tenement, motto, ethnic group, immigrant, immigrate, citizen

were the five most common labels given to the words (or whatever number is appropriate for the subject you are studying), and use those as the main labels on the word wall. Students can then use note cards and a marker to create a spot for the words. Stop weekly to examine the word wall and add new words that have come up in the reading, adjust the labels if students think of better ones, and even remove words that are not important.

Updated Strategy #2: Developing Whole-Class Word Wall Strategies

Your wall is up—congratulations! Now it is time to make sure your wall is in constant use by highlighting the words on the wall with a variety of strategies. Whole-class strategies, like those presented in this section, are great for days when you have a few extra minutes at the end of class. Chapter 8 is dedicated to these activities; those presented here pertain only to the word wall.

♦ **Baseball** (Tunkel, 2012): The baseball word wall activity was inspired by a kindergarten teacher. She divided her class into teams and called up students to the plate to "bat," which entailed reading a word from the word wall. If they read it correctly, they took a base. As other students came up to bat, students moved along the bases until they were brought home by their teammates. If a student read the word incorrectly, that was an out.

To update this strategy for middle and high school students, still divide the class into teams. Have a pile of the word wall words in front of you, the umpire. Students step up to bat like Babe Ruth and call their shots, moving right up Bloom's Taxonomy:

Single: spell the word

Double: spell the word and give a definition (recall)

Triple: spell the word, give a definition, and use the word correctly in a creative sentence (recall and application)

Home run: do all the above plus make a connection between the word and another word being studied (recall, application, and synthesis)

A student who misses any part of his or her called "shot" is out. Students move along the bases and score when they are brought "home" by their own home run or a teammate's "hit." Baseball can be played over multiple periods!

♦ **The Chain:** More than just a song by Fleetwood Mac, the Chain is a great way to highlight connections among words as a unit progresses. Present each student with one word from the word wall on a card. Students read their cards aloud to the class so that everyone knows who has what. Ask each student to consider his or her word relative to other students' words, and then ask if one student will self-nominate as the central idea for the unit being studied. There can be some significant wait time as students look at their cards, their neighbors' cards, and then over their course materials before one student (often prodded by peers) raises his or her hand as the central idea. This student stands in the middle of the classroom. From there, students again self-nominate to join the central idea. In order to create the chain, they must explain their relationship to the central idea, how they are connected. Slowly but surely, every student with a card builds off others standing, until a complicated chain of words and ideas is created around the classroom. More creative students will make rationales for standing in front of, behind, or on either side of a concept, showing relationships with multiple dimensions. If desired, the cards can be rearranged on the word wall to reflect "The Chain" that was just built during this word wall strategy.

♦ **Which Word Is Missing?** For a quick word wall strategy, Which Word Is Missing? can't be beat. This is a great way to see how much attention students have been paying to the word wall. During independent or small-group instructional time, remove one card from the wall, arranging the cards so that the missing space is covered (or pull one word off the wall before class starts). Right before the bell, ask students to consider the word wall. Tell them one word is missing, and watch as they read the words over and over again, trying to figure out which one is gone. Prompt students to go back to course materials, or where the word wall word came from in the first place, to see if they can figure out which important concept is missing. Sooner or later, someone figures it out. This is a great activity if you have two minutes before the bell rings!

Updated Strategy #3: Developing Small-Group Word Wall Strategies

The following strategies work particularly well with small groups or partners to highlight words on the word walls. The Chain can also be done in small groups; instead of distributing one card per student, place students in groups of three or four and give them a small stack of words (no more than ten) to create a concept chain that they will have to explain to the rest of the class.

♦ **Compare/Contrast:** Identifying similarities and differences between vocabulary words is a great way for students to work new words into their schema. In this strategy, randomly give two students two cards. Using a Venn diagram, the students first list in the circles characteristics that the words do not share and then work to find commonalities to list in the overlapping space. An example of a Venn diagram comparing two of the words from the List-Group-Label on immigration is in Figure 7.2.

♦ **Word Wall Words in Writing** (Callella, 2001): This strategy can be done in partners or individually. Depending on the amount of time you have designated for this strategy, decide how many word wall words you would like

Figure 7.2 Venn Diagram with Two Immigration Words

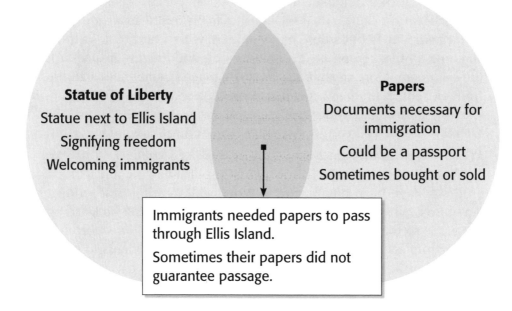

Statue of Liberty
Statue next to Ellis Island
Signifying freedom
Welcoming immigrants

Papers
Documents necessary for immigration
Could be a passport
Sometimes bought or sold

Immigrants needed papers to pass through Ellis Island.
Sometimes their papers did not guarantee passage.

students to include in a short writing piece. You can simply set a number, or you can remove cards from the word wall and distribute them to partners or individuals. Ask students to create a story or write a paragraph using that number of words correctly. This is a great formative or summative assessment that allows you to see student application of words in context.

♦ **Walking the Wall** (Graves & Watts-Taffe, 2008): This strategy can be done independently or in pairs. As the word wall grows, students should be encouraged to interact with it personally. Leave a stack of sticky notes in front of the wall, and when time allows, students can "walk the wall," adding synonyms and antonyms to words, personal reactions to words ("I like this word because …"), adding related words, etc.

Common Core Connection

Word walls are a great way to get students working toward mastery of the anchor vocabulary standards in the Common Core State Standards, as shown in Figure 7.3.

Figure 7.3   Common Core State Standards

Grade Level	4	5	6
Standard Addressed	**Language Standard** Acquire and use accurately grade-appropriate general academic and domain-specific words and phrases, including those that signal precise actions, emotions, or states of being (e.g., *quizzed, whined, stammered*) and that are basic to a particular topic (e.g., *wildlife, conservation,* and *endangered* when discussing animal preservation).	**Language Standard** Acquire and use accurately grade-appropriate general academic and domain-specific words and phrases, including those that signal contrast, addition, and other logical relation-ships (e.g., *however, although, nevertheless, similarly, moreover, in addition*).	**Language Standard** Acquire and use accurately grade-appropriate general academic and domain-specific words and phrases; gather vocabulary knowledge when considering a word or phrase important to comprehension or expression.

(Continued)

Grade Level	7	8	9–10
Standard Addressed	**Language Standard** Acquire and use accurately grade-appropriate general academic and domain-specific words and phrases; gather vocabulary knowledge when considering a word or phrase important to comprehension or expression.	**Language Standard** Acquire and use accurately grade-appropriate general academic and domain-specific words and phrases; gather vocabulary knowledge when considering a word or phrase important to comprehension or expression.	**Language Standard** Acquire and use accurately general academic and domain-specific words and phrases, sufficient for reading, writing, speaking, and listening at the college and career readiness level; demonstrate independence in gathering vocabulary knowledge when considering a word or phrase important to comprehension or expression.

Source: NGAC/CCSSO, 2010

Action Steps

I hope this chapter has helped you build the capacity to create an interactive and fully functional word wall in your own classroom. Take some action:

1. What type of word wall will work best in your classroom? Why?

   _____

   _____

2. Develop a plan for building your word wall. Will you choose the words at first? Or will you allow students to brainstorm words around categories?

   _____

   _____

3. Where will your word wall go?

   _____

   _____

4. Select a word wall strategy to work into your word study routine and try it with students.

    a. Which one did you choose? Why?

    _____

    _____

    b. Did the strategy you chose help reinforce word learning in your classroom? How do you know?

    _____

    _____

5. CHALLENGE: Try List-Group-Label with your students at the beginning of a unit. After trying the strategy out, REFLECT:

    Did students brainstorm the words you had in mind?

_____

_____

_____

_____

Chapter 8

Use and Apply Vocabulary Words Regularly
(versus Isolated Practice)

Mr. Lowe was the English teacher during my junior year of high school. He had a reputation as a strict teacher, but seniors told my classmates and me that we would leave as better readers and writers. For two weeks, we sat in class, afraid to say a word. In the third week, my friend Stacey raised her hand. "Mr. Lowe," she said, "you have that word above the chalkboard, ambivalence. Why is it up there, and what does it mean?" He smiled at her with a Cheshire cat grin. "Stacey, I have been waiting since the beginning of school for one of you to notice that word and ask me about it. That shows intellectual curiosity. You are starting us off on our year's exploration of interesting and expressive words that we can use in writing and conversation. We will begin with the word above the board, ambivalence."

Why This Item Is Important

I encourage teachers to support their students in becoming collectors of words. "Marinating" in language, I call it, giving the students the opportunity not only to notice new and fun words but also to try them out—to play, practice, and manipulate the words until they ultimately become their own. "I don't have time to allow my students to 'marinate,'" one teacher told me at a professional development workshop. "We are short-order cooks at my school. I need them to get the concept so we can move on to other important concepts."

The strategies presented in this section are "nook-and-cranny" strategies. Understanding the unwieldy curriculum that teachers masterfully map out to teach, I became a collector of strategies that take five or fewer minutes to implement into the classroom. When you have a few minutes left at the end of class, when you might let students begin homework or chat—why not turn these moments into word play?

Understand that these strategies are in addition to the planned teaching of vocabulary words that are important to concepts. Instead, these strategies encourage students to use increasingly sophisticated words in their writing and speaking—just as Mr. Lowe did with us.

> **Do This–Not That** principle #8: **DO** find creative ways to engage students in word study all the time; **DON'T** isolate vocabulary study only to language arts time.

Updated Strategy #1: Using Golden Words/Phrases

When you walk into Casey Oberhauser's seventh-grade language arts classroom, the first thing you notice is the writing on the windows. No, her students are not defacing school property; they are constantly combing through their independent reading selections for golden words and phrases. In order to create a print-rich environment (Allington & Cunningham, 2006; Vacca, Vacca, Gove, et al., 2011), Casey Oberhauser took advantage of the windows in her room. "It was the one space I hadn't tried to turn into something usable," she said. "And I knew the students would love writing on the windows." To prepare for the strategy, Casey purchases Crayola window crayons.

During the first few days of school when she is doing a read aloud of the *Hunger Games* (Collins, 2009), she models coming across a word that sparks her interest. She stops after the word *squat*. "Did you notice this word?" she'll prompt her students. "That qualifies as a "Golden Word." Mouths open, the students watch as she takes a glass marker and writes the word on the window. "If you come across a great word or phrase in your reading, you can write it on the window when we are finished with our self-selected reading time."

All year, students carefully read their books, finding words to add to the windows. If time allows, Casey stops before the bell rings to draw student attention to the windows and ask about the context of the word and why it was chosen.

Updated Strategy #2: Introducing Word Jars (Barger, 2006)

As a literacy coach, I often model lessons in classrooms. I end up with a few moments left at the end of my demonstration where the students, the teacher, and I will sit awkwardly, waiting for the bell to ring. The Word Jar strategy became my favorite way to fill these moments.

Three containers become my Word Jars (coffee cans work best because of the lids). I cover and label each jar with a different phrase:

1. Words that tickle my ears

2. Words that warm my heart

3. Words that make me feel smarter

These labels work well with primary students; for older students, I might use more-sophisticated labels:

1. Onomatopoeia

2. Words that evoke emotion

3. Intelligent words

During my first demonstration lesson, I introduce the concept of the Word Jars to the students. I ask them to collect words for me during the week, writing them on notecards and inserting them into the slot I cut into the top of the coffee can lid. I model words for them in each category: *ooze* for the first category, *contentment* for the second, and *ponder* for the third. I leave the jars in the classroom, and during my weekly visits, I purposely leave a few minutes at the end of the lesson to go through the jars to see what words the students collected for me. I pull a few out, inviting the students who submitted the words to tell the class and me where they found the words and why they like them. We can then add these words to the word wall in the classroom.

Updated Strategy #3: Using Vocabulary Tableaux (Rasinski, 2003; Tortello, 2004; Wilhelm, 2002)

Tableau is best described as still charades. It was originally conceived as a comprehension strategy, where students use their bodies in snapshots of events of a text; small groups of students work together to create their snapshot of this event and "strike a pose" in front of the class. The class works to figure out which scene is being depicted, and the teacher can animate students to discuss their role in the scene with a tap on the shoulder.

Vocabulary tableaux came about after a discussion with a teacher who described her room full of kinesthetic learners. "We do a lot of charades," she explained, "but it is getting old. How else can they learn vocabulary with their bodies?"

To bring vocabulary to life, I carefully selected words from the content the class was studying, the food chain. I divided the class into groups of two or three and handed each group a word on a card. I then modeled the strategy for them: I showed them that my word was *energy*. We brainstormed various ways I could show this word without moving: putting my arms out to show I was the sun and holding a still runner's pose were two suggestions by the class. I took my pose, and the students agreed that it showed energy without moving. Next, they went to work on their words: *herbivores, carnivores, omnivores*, and *decomposers* were examples of the words they used. Students were given three minutes to create their word pictures. Groups of students posed, and the rest of the class tried to guess which word they were creating. For *carnivore*, one student got down on all fours and stuck his hand up behind his head to show a lion's mane. He opened his mouth as if to bite his partner, who had covered himself with a green tablecloth (props are allowed). If we got stuck, I would tap individuals on the shoulder, and they could give clues about what word their bodies were depicting.

This strategy takes time to flow. However, when students get the basics down, it becomes a great active nook-and-cranny activity. A different tableau can be called each day to illustrate a word of interest.

Updated Strategy #4: Celebrating Word of the Week (Fisher & Frey, 2008)

Word of the Week is not a new concept. My own iteration of this strategy was used with English language learners in a middle school in East Los Angeles. My students struggled with vocabulary as a whole, but they were especially challenged with vocabulary in literature. A previous teacher had trained them to look up unknown words, so my students stopped every sentence or so to look up a word, completely losing their comprehension of the text along the way. There was no feasible way to teach them every unknown word in a text; Allen (2008) points out that an expert teacher can teach only about 350 words a year to students, and I was more focused on survival vocabulary for my students, many of whom were new to this country. Yet I still wanted them to experience the richness of the English language. I stumbled across www.allwords.com. On the left-hand side of the Web site is a link labeled Word of the Week. Each week, the Web site presents a new word of the week, complete with definitions and usage.

The strategy worked like this: Each week, a student was designated the Word Master. He or she got to sit at my desk and use my computer to research the word of the week from the Web site. The Word Master then briefly conferred with me to check pronunciation and meaning. The student was in charge of introducing the word to the class with a brief "word talk," sharing the meaning and an example of how it could be used in a sentence. The word was displayed above the board in large letters for everyone to see, along with a two- to three-word definition.

The Word Master was then in charge of the word for the week. Every time the rest of the class was able to work the word into class discussion, the Word Master made a tally mark on a card and, if possible, wrote down the sentence and context in which it was used. On Friday, before the bell rang, the Word Master reported to the class how many times students were able to use the word and shared a few of the instances it was used in conversation. The word then was taken off the board and posted around the perimeter of the room, with the tally card below it. By the end of the year, students were able to see the new words they had added to their vocabulary and compare which words were easy and challenging to use in class discussion.

Common Core Connection

Encouraging students to acquire and use a variety of words across contexts is included in the Common Core State Standards for the English Language Arts. These standards are summarized in Figure 8.1 on page 102.

Figure 8.1 Common Core State Standards

Grade Level	4	5	6
Standard Addressed	**Language Standard** Acquire and use accurately grade-appropriate general academic and domain-specific words and phrases, including those that signal precise actions, emotions, or states of being (e.g., *quizzed, whined, stammered*) and that are basic to a particular topic (e.g., *wildlife, conservation,* and *endangered* when discussing animal preservation).	**Language Standard** Acquire and use accurately grade-appropriate general academic and domain-specific words and phrases, including those that signal contrast, addition, and other logical relation-ships (e.g., *however, although, nevertheless, similarly, moreover, in addition*).	**Language Standard** Acquire and use accurately grade-appropriate general academic and domain-specific words and phrases; gather vocabulary knowledge when considering a word or phrase important to comprehension or expression.
Grade Level	**7**	**8**	**9–10**
Standard Addressed	**Language Standard** Acquire and use accurately grade-appropriate general academic and domain-specific words and phrases; gather vocabulary knowledge when considering a word or phrase important to comprehension or expression.	**Language Standard** Acquire and use accurately grade-appropriate general academic and domain-specific words and phrases; gather vocabulary knowledge when considering a word or phrase important to comprehension or expression.	**Language Standard** Acquire and use accurately general academic and domain-specific words and phrases, sufficient for read-ing, writing, speak-ing, and listening at the college and career readiness level; demonstrate independence in gathering vocabu-lary knowledge when considering a word or phrase important to comprehension or expression.

Action Steps

The "short-order" cook from the introduction of this section wrote me an e-mail a few months after our professional development workshop. She gave me permission to share a piece of it here: "OK, these strategies have been a lot of fun. The students yell at me if I forget about Word of the Week. I guess I am progressing toward the Slow Food Movement from my position in a diner!" I hope these strategies will encourage you and your students to "marinate" in language, too. Take some action:

1. In Chapter 2, we discussed building routines in the classroom for deep word instruction. The nook-and-cranny strategies discussed in this section can also become a routine for those empty moments in your classroom. Choose one strategy—Golden Words, Word Jars, Word of the Day, or Vocabulary Tableaux—and plan to set it up as a routine in your classroom.

    a. REFLECT: Which strategy did you choose? Why?

    _____

    _____

    b. Plan for introducing this strategy to your students: When will you model it for them? How will you ensure that it continues throughout the week or unit of study?

    _____

    _____

    _____

    c. Keep the strategy going for a month or so. How successful was the implementation? Are you ready to change it or continue on with this strategy?

    _____

    _____

    _____

Chapter 9

Allow Opportunities for Wide Reading so Students Are Exposed to Words All the Time in a Variety of Books

I was invited to watch a group of tenth graders present creative book reports at a local school. As the "judge," I got to say who did the best job "selling" his or her book to the rest of the class, and I watched in delight as students had three minutes to give their best for the prize (a Barnes and Noble gift card). Second to last was Darren, a student I had had in another district as part of a small group of gifted students once a week. Darren was immensely creative, and I knew his presentation would be excellent. He got up in front of the class and read a poem about a book that instantly rang a bell with its familiarity in my head. His poem was good, but it wasn't the caliber I had expected, and I awarded the prize to a student who had done slam poetry about Unwind, by Neal Shusterman. I pulled Darren aside after the competition was over. "Darren," I asked while he looked down at his shoes, "didn't you read that book with me in sixth grade? I seem to remember you talking about it in our group." He glanced up at me and grinned. "Dr. Wilfong, I've been giving the same book report for five years now. No one checks or anything. And it was a hard book for a sixth grader."

Why This Item Is Important

Although this item is number nine on the list, it is not diminished in importance. Creating and nurturing independent reading in a variety of texts is the single most important thing a teacher can do to create a classroom of wordsmiths (Allen, 2007; Ivey & Broaddus, 2007; Krashen, 1993; Lapp, Fisher, & Jacobson, 2008; Nagy, 1988; Ohanian, 2006). Independent reading allows for students to grow their vocabularies incidentally, letting them reach beyond the words a teacher can directly instruct daily to reach their potential for comprehension and vocabulary expansion (Allen, 2007). A widely cited study by Nagy & Anderson (1984) illustrates this point: Students will come in contact with 88,500 word families by the time they complete high school. This can be worked out to roughly 500,000 individual words. Fisher and Frey (2008) divided that number by half to try to make it more manageable but then showed that if students need to know 250,000 over the 13 years they are in school, at 180 days a year, then they need to learn 107 words a day (without absences!).

Because we know that six to eight words a week is roughly the amount a teacher should focus on for direct instruction, reading must be counted on to help make up the difference. And independent reading is best, giving students the chance to read and use their newly acquired strategies to attack and conquer unknown words in context (Allen, 2007; Beers, 2002).

> **Do This–Not That** principle #9: **DO** find time in your classroom to allow students to read interesting and appropriate texts on both subject matter (bounded choice) and subjects of interests (self-selected). **DON'T** pick everything that students read, and don't read everything aloud to students!

To Get Started

Content area teachers often balk at the idea of allowing time for students to read independently for a variety of reasons. Let's dispel these myths right away:

- *The textbooks (or other curriculum materials) are too hard for the kids.* This is the statement I hear when teachers are trying to rationalize the fact that they read every piece of material aloud to their students. What they don't realize is they are creating an atmosphere of dependency by doing this; students will quickly learn that they never need to do the work themselves.

- *There isn't enough time to allow students to read independently.* When teachers are planning instruction and running short on time, time to read texts independently is often the first thing to go. One teacher explained it to me like this: "If I give time for them to read the text themselves, so many of them take too long. It is easier just to put the audio of the book on and know I can finish in a set amount of time." I was able to convince this teacher that she had to start letting students read independently because that is the type of reading that is done on standardized tests.

♦ *Allowing students to independently read is not teaching.* This is one idea that teachers and administrators both need to get over. I have been a part of many walk-throughs where the administrative team walks into a room of quiet readers, and the teacher gets a look of panic on his or her face. Such teachers feel that if they are not active in their instruction (literally up in front of the students), they are not actually teaching. This has to be dispelled. Allowing the students to independently try out their newly acquired strategies is the ultimate in teaching!

Updated Strategy #1: Setting Up for Effective Self-Selected Reading

When we hear the term *self-selected reading*, we might picture the SSR of old: students reading at their desks for a set amount of time, often with little accountability for what they read. Silent Sustained Reading, or SSR, always sounded like jail to me: you must be SILENT, you must SUSTAIN, and you will READ. No wonder so many teachers and students loathed this time!

As you consider how to effectively put independent reading into your classroom, plan for the following: time, texts, and tasks. These three "Ts" are loosely based on the six Ts of Effective Instruction developed by Allington (2002).

1. **Time:** Allington (2002) points out that exemplary teachers find time in their classrooms for all students to read and write as much as possible. Examine a typical day in your classroom. Where can time spent on housekeeping and transitions be minimized? If daily independent reading is not possible (although highly recommended), then how many days of the week can you devote to reading? If time was previously spent on reading the text aloud to students, begin by replacing that time with time spent independently reading.

   Allen (2007) makes a compelling push for time spent reading: Most students need to read for 25 minutes a day to maintain their reading levels. However, students who are two or more grade levels below their grade placement need to read for 90 minutes or more a day to begin to catch up. Where can you "catch" those minutes for such students?

Teachers often tell me they assign independent reading for homework, either from curriculum materials or choice texts, and then complain that this reading is never completed. Atwell (1998; 2007), a reading workshop advocate and independent reading professional, gives compelling reasons for letting students read in class. She firmly believes that reading creates readers, but simply assigning reading for homework, without letting students develop as readers in class, will not do the trick. If they read in front of you, in class, you know they are reading (or at least, they are doing a good job faking it). Then that time spent reading in class will pay off with students wanting to read outside of class!

2. **Texts:** For language arts teachers, the importance of matching students with appropriate-level texts and interesting content cannot be underestimated. You might be one of the few people in a student's life who takes an interest in that student as a reader; figuring out what books are right for that student, both in level and content, is paramount for the student in learning how to self-select books. In language arts, independently read texts should be self-selected; the student is getting a chance to learn vocabulary and practice comprehension strategies in a book of his or her choice.

   For content area teachers, texts used to be one-note: the textbook or curriculum materials the district provides. But as discussed above, mandated curriculum materials are often difficult or boring or both. It was also traditional for content area teachers to view texts to teach concepts as a one-stop shop; one text was used for everyone. But as classrooms have become more diverse, it makes sense to differentiate the texts. This can work as follows: Select a topic of study. Using a variety of resources and with knowledge of the abilities of your students, you may select several texts around this topic. Distribute texts purposely (matching text level with student ability), or allow students to choose a text from a selection you have culled (bounded choice). Figure 9.1 gives several resources to find texts on a variety of subjects and levels.

3. **Tasks:** What you ask students to do with the texts is crucial to building student capacity as readers and writers. Allington (2002) points to the worksheets teachers often assign as assessment; there is very little teaching associated with a student's reading a passage and then

Figure 9.1   Resources for Quality, Differentiated Texts

Source	Description	Differentiation
Time for Kids www.time-forkids.com	*Time for Kids* is an offshoot of the adult *Time* magazine. Published weekly, *Time for Kids* reports on timely and current issues affecting the world from a student's point of view.	This resource is published at four different levels: K-1, 2, 3-4, and 5-6. The same topics are covered at the various levels, allowing for students to read the same information but presented appropriately.
Primary Search Plus, EBSCO-host database	This database, found through the EBSCOhost search engine, is geared toward elementary-aged readers. Type in a subject and find thousands of free fiction and nonfiction texts centering on that topic. Most articles are offered in HTML or pdf format.	The database is searchable by Lexile (reading level); several articles on the same topic can be found on different reading levels. You can read texts found in HTML format to students, if necessary.
Middle Search Plus, EBSCO-host database	This database, found through the EBSCOhost search engine, is geared toward middle school–aged readers. Type in a subject and find thousands of free fiction and nonfiction texts centering on that topic. Most articles are offered in HTML or pdf format.	The database is searchable by Lexile (reading level); several articles on the same topic can be found on different reading levels. You can read texts found in HTML format to students, if necessary.

filling out a comprehension worksheet. Instead, students need to be asked to apply their new knowledge meaningfully; Updated Strategy #2 discusses three ways to help students use their independently read texts to amplify vocabulary learning.

To check for comprehension in meaningful ways, consider using the following two strategies:

a. The Most Important Thing

The Important Book, by Margaret Wise Brown (1990), is a great way to model simple summary writing for students. Each two-page spread of the book gives the "important thing" about a subject: daisies, rain, spoons, etc. Each spread follows the template used in Figure 9.2 on page 110.

Figure 9.2 Most Important Thing Template

The important thing about _____ is _____.
Detail #1 _____
Detail #2 _____
Detail #3 _____
But the important thing about _____ is _____.

A full-size template of this summary strategy is on page 116. After students have read a text independently, they can fill out this template to show what they thought was the most important thing they read about. It provides great formative assessment! An example of a filled-out Important Thing template is shown in Figure 9.3.

Figure 9.3 Completed Most Important Thing Template

The most important thing about *the Civil War* is *that it was a war between the States.*
The North wanted to abolish slavery.
The South wanted to preserve its way of life.
The war resulted in slavery being abolished and the United States remaining unified.
But the most important thing about *the Civil War* is *that it was a war between the States.*

  b. Final Countdown
    More than an '80s song, the Final Countdown allows students to recall facts, ask questions, and make connections between the text they are reading and their other learning. The blank template is in Figure 9.4 and included in full-size on page 115.
    Again, after students have read a text, they can complete the Final Countdown template to help them organize their learning.

Updated Strategy #2: Using Independent Reading Purposely to Amplify Vocabulary Learning

Now that you have students reading a variety of texts independently in your classroom, it is time to connect that reading back to their vocabulary learning.

Figure 9.4 Final Countdown Template

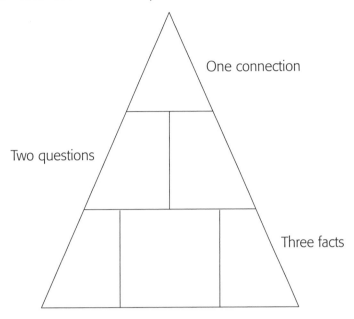

Below is a list of strategies that will help you emphasize word study during this time.

♦ Independently read texts can easily be connected back to the word wall:

1. *Provide space to recognize the context of a word being used.* Find wall space near your word wall for students to display words found in their reading that are also found on the word wall. Keep a stack of sticky notes near the word wall, and when students come across a word wall word in their reading, have them copy the sentence onto a note. See how many you can gather over the duration of that word wall.

2. *Ask students to nominate new words from their reading for the word wall.* Bromley (2003) used a brief amount of time after independent reading for students to add new and interesting words to the word wall.

♦ Have students keep a section of a reader response journal devoted to word study. In this section, they can record new words they come across while reading. Remind students to add to this list periodically.

♦ Go outside the word wall or teacher-selected words of study; have students participate in strategies (like those from Chapter 2) on words they choose from their independent text.

- Use an adapted version of the Reader's Chair at the conclusion of independent reading time (Routman, 2002). In the traditional use of the strategy, students sit in a special chair and describe their reading to the class. To highlight vocabulary words, ask students to volunteer to share with the class a word they found interesting, puzzling, or unfamiliar from their independent reading.

- Ask students to contribute to your Word Jars (Chapter 8) at the conclusion of independent reading.

- Ask students to identify a word with a Greek or Latin root in their independent reading (Chapter 5). Have them create a word tree for the root, brainstorming other words that share that same root, prefix, or suffix.

Common Core Connection

Reading and vocabulary acquisition is specifically addressed in the Reading Standards for Literature and Reading Standards for Informational Text, shown in Figure 9.5.

Figure 9.5 Common Core State Standards

Grade Level	4	5	6
Standard Addressed	**Reading Standard for Literature** Determine the meaning of words and phrases as they are used in a text, including those that allude to significant characters found in mythology (e.g., *Herculean*). **Reading Standard for Informational Text** Determine the meaning of general academic and domain-specific words and phrases in a text relevant to a *grade 4 topic or subject area.*	**Reading Standard for Literature** Determine the meaning of words and phrases as they are used in a text, including figurative language such as metaphors and similes. **Reading Standard for Informational Text** Determine the meaning of general academic and domain-specific words and phrases in a text relevant to a *grade 5 topic or subject area.*	**Reading Standard for Literature** Determine the meaning of words and phrases as they are used in a text, including figurative and connotative meanings; analyze the impact of a specific word choice on meaning and tone. **Reading Standard for Informational Text** Determine the meaning of words and phrases as they are used in a text, including figurative, connotative, and technical meanings.

Grade Level	7	8	9
Standard Addressed	**Reading Standard for Literature** Determine the meaning of words and phrases as they are used in a text, including figurative and connotative meanings; analyze the impact of rhymes and other repetitions of sounds (e.g., alliteration) on a specific verse or stanza of a poem or section of a story or drama. **Reading Standard for Informational Text** Determine the meaning of words and phrases as they are used in a text, including figurative, connotative, and technical meanings; analyze the impact of a specific word choice on meaning and tone.	**Reading Standard for Literature** Determine the meaning of words and phrases as they are used in a text, including figurative and connotative meanings; analyze the impact of specific word choices on meaning and tone, including analogies or allusions to other texts. **Reading Standard for Informational Text** Determine the meaning of words and phrases as they are used in a text, including figurative, connotative, and technical meanings; analyze the impact of specific word choices on meaning and tone, including analogies or allusions to other texts.	**Reading Standard for Literature** Determine the meaning of words and phrases as they are used in the text, including figurative and connotative meanings; analyze the cumulative impact of specific word choices on meaning and tone (e.g., how the language evokes a sense of time and place; how it sets a formal or informal tone). **Reading Standard for Informational Text** Determine the meaning of words and phrases as they are used in a text, including figurative, connotative, and technical meanings; analyze the cumulative impact of specific word choices on meaning and tone (e.g., how the language of a court opinion differs from that of a newspaper).

Source: NGAC/CCSSO, 2010

Action Steps

Incorporating independent reading into your classroom takes some of the direct instruction burden off your shoulders when it comes to vocabulary. It effectively adds to your word study routine by giving students time to apply and practice word attack skills in appropriate text while building student vocabularies through incidental learning. Take some action:

1. Brainstorm three ways you can find more time in your classroom to fit in independent reading:

   a. _____

   _____

   b. _____

   _____

   c. _____

   _____

2. Try out one of the resources mentioned in Figure 9.1 to find new and differentiated texts to provide bounded choice for your students.

   a. What subject did you search? _____

   b. How many articles did you find? _____

   c. Out of all those articles, which activities could you actually use with your students?

   _____

   _____

3. Select one of the six strategies mentioned in Updated Strategy #2 to use with your students after their independent reading.

   REFLECT: Which did you choose? Why?

   _____

   _____

   _____

   _____

   _____

   _____

Final Countdown

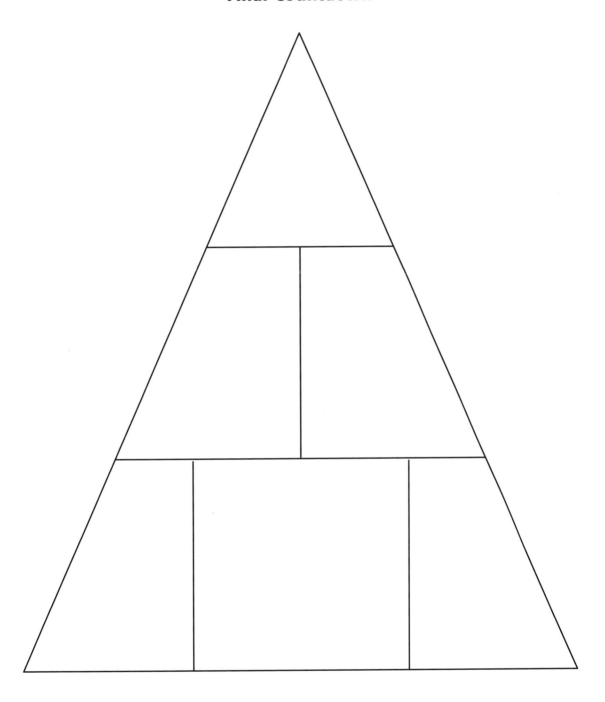

The Most Important Thing

Name: _____ Date _____

The important thing about …
Summarize your learning by stating the most important thing you learned about a subject. Follow that statement with three more sentences containing three different facts about that subject. Finish by repeating the first sentence again.

1. The important thing about _____ is

2. _____

   _____

   _____

   _____

3. _____

   _____

   _____

   _____

4. _____

   _____

   _____

   _____

5. But the important thing about _____ is

   _____

   _____

   _____

   _____

   _____

Model the Use of Academic Language at All Times, Setting High Expectations for Language Use

My colleague Rachel is a Title I reading teacher in an urban school district, and from day one in her classroom, she holds all students who walk through her door accountable for the language they speak. She begins gently, helping students reach for new words to replace the language they use in their everyday life. For example, when a student asks to use "it," when they need to use the restroom, instead of mocking them by asking, "Use what?" she reminds them that in this room, they ask to use the facilities. Slowly but surely, students grow into this new role of sophisticated language, and by midyear, a kindergartner will say in the sweetest of voices: "I'm parched. May I refresh myself at the drinking fountain?" She always laughs and says, "How can I refuse you when you ask so well?"

Why This Item Is Important

Teachers today have more higher education than ever before. In my home state of Ohio, teachers are required to get a master's degree within seven years of getting their first position in a school; most teachers go on for a "master's plus" for the love of learning more about their craft. Yet language in the classroom has disintegrated as teachers try to reach students: "I can't use big words," one teacher confided in me. "The kids do not have any idea what I am saying." As possibly the most learned person your students come into contact with on a regular basis, you owe your own use of academic language to them (or at least to the financial aid officer who holds your debt). Chatting with students about after-school activities or what's for lunch is fine for everyday language, but as soon as academics begin, so should the use of academic language (Lane & Allen, 2010).

> **Do This–Not That** principle #10: **DO** build the capacity in your students to reach for and understand a variety of words so that they sound like the scholars you are encouraging them to become; **DON'T** allow students to slacken their language use around you in the classroom!

To Get Started

Payne (2005) describes the registers of speech that we need to explicitly teach all students. The registers are the key for clarifying for students when and where it is OK to speak (or write) casually and when and where a more formal voice is necessary. Figure 10.1 shows these registers.

Figure 10.1   Registers of Language

Register	Description/Characteristics
Frozen	Language is always the same; used in ceremonial settings (Catholic mass and weddings)
Formal	Newscasts, workplace meetings, school setting; characterized by complete sentences and selective word use
Consultative	Conversations of people interacting in formal situations (school, work)
Casual	Interactions between friends and family; general word choice, often shorter sentences
Intimate	Conversations between lovers and twins

These registers can be the key to the "hidden rules" for students when it comes to working more sophisticated language into their speech and writing at school. Many students do not know that it is not OK to say "This sucks" to a teacher, because no one has previously told them it is inappropriate.

Most teachers get angry at this type of speech in the classroom, but rather than choosing anger, tell students what your expectation of language is in the classroom. This doesn't have to be a long conversation or lesson; instead, present the registers quickly, and set out the register expected in school (Formal/Consultative).

Graves &Watts-Taffe (2008) advocate for read alouds as a great jumping off point for incorporating new words into a classroom. Choosing read alouds with specific vocabulary to highlight helps work new words naturally into students' consciousness.

Updated Strategy #1: Speaking Academic Language in School

At a school where I had a long-standing consultancy, we adopted a yearlong exploration into the use of academic language. It began at the front door; as soon as people walked up the steps and through the main door, they saw a banner hanging above the stairwell that proclaimed, "Academic language spoken here." Students knew the moment they came into the building that their talk must be elevated.

We started small, using a list by Costa and Marzano (2001) of precise versus non-precise talk (Figure 10.2). As teachers, we decided to replace our nonprecise language with language that said exactly what we meant, an important aspect of language use with a high-poverty student population (Costa & Marzano, 2001).

Figure 10.2 Precise versus Nonprecise Talk

Nonprecise	Precise
Look at …	*Compare* these …
What will happen … ?	*Predict* what will happen … .
Place into groups …	*Classify* …
Work this problem …	*Analyze* this problem …
What do you think … ?	What *conclusions* do you come to … ?
How do you explain … ?	What *hypotheses* explain … ?

These were easy replacements for the teachers, but we found early on that they had to be visible for teachers to use them effectively in their own instruction. So we developed teacher word walls. Visible mainly to a teacher, either at the back of the room in the sight line of the teacher, or as a small, laminated note card the teacher could hold, the word wall became a constant reminder to use precise language in the classroom.

My personal nemesis in precise language is the saying "Eyes on me." My cooperating teacher during student teaching called the class back together by counting down from three, and then the teacher and the students would chant together, "Eyes on me" (teacher) or "Eyes on you" (student). It was catchy and effective but completely imprecise; did I literally mean that I wanted students to pop out their eyeballs and put them on me? (Um, no) So I started counting down from three and saying, "Focus on me." It worked just as well and was a quick and easy tweak to my own language in the classroom.

We then invited students into our academic language initiative. We asked students in small groups to brainstorm things that they said all the time that lacked in academic sophistication or precise language. Students enthusiastically produced the following list of sayings:

- I'm bored./This sucks.

- Do we have homework?

- Will this be on the test?

- Is there extra credit?

- He/She is touching/bothering/looking at me.

This list made us laugh because it very closely mirrored our own list of things we would like to change about the students' speech in class! We then got out the thesauruses. We asked students to work together to come up with more sophisticated, precise, and academic ways to say these sayings. Figure 10.3 shows their replacements.

Some of the replacement sayings got pretty extreme, and yet the students were so into them! We hung these sheets on the wall, and the students agreed that if they felt the need to say any of the original sayings (all of which were pointed out to belong to the more casual register), they would replace it with the more formal, academic saying.

We then turned the tables on the teachers. The students brainstormed things their teachers said all the time:

- Take out your book/pencil/pen/paper.

- Stop talking.

- Line up.

- Hands and feet to yourself.

- No talking in the hallway.

The thesauruses came out again and students brainstormed ways to assist their teachers in sounding more academic and formal. Their list is in Figure 10.4.

Figure 10.3 Replacements for Student Casual Speech

Original saying	Academic language
I'm bored./This sucks.	◆ This no longer interests me. ◆ My interest in learning has waned. ◆ May I explore a different topic? ◆ May I explore this topic differently? ◆ Perhaps my learning style is not suited to this particular activity.
Do we have homework?	◆ Do we have an opportunity to extend our learning this evening? ◆ Will this task require work in my residence? ◆ May I terminate this task in my habitat?
Will this be on the test?	◆ Will I need to demonstrate my knowledge of this pearl of wisdom on the assessment? ◆ Will this learning appear on the assessment?
Is there extra credit?	◆ May I earn additional points? ◆ May I dazzle you with my knowledge of this topic on a nonrequired assignment?
He/she is bothering/touching/looking at me.	◆ A fellow classmate is disturbing my learning. ◆ My peer will not allow me to extend my knowledge of this topic.

Figure 10.4 Replacements for Teacher Casual Speech

Original saying	Academic language
Take out your book/pencil/pen/paper.	◆ Retrieve your tome/writing utensil/papyrus. ◆ Take out the necessary learning paraphernalia.
Stop talking.	◆ Cease speaking. ◆ Terminate the conversation.
Line up	◆ Arrange yourselves in a linear fashion.
Hands and feet to yourself.	◆ Retain control of your limbs. ◆ Do not allow your extremities to wander.
No talking in the hallway.	◆ Cease the discourse on the concourse.

Just as we did with the student sayings, we posted these in the classroom, and the teachers committed to using the academic language the students created. This set the tone for an entire year of using precise and academic language in the classroom. As one teacher reported, "I think this gave permission for students to sound smart in my classroom. One student didn't stand out for using big words; they all were using big words."

Updated Strategy #2: Interpreting Shades of Meaning

Getting students to replace everyday speech with more academic language is a step in the right direction; getting students to think about the descriptors they use in their speech and writing is the next step. Graves & Watts-Taffe (2008) mention an English teacher who asks his students to go through an essay and replace common adjectives with more interesting words through the use of a thesaurus. This teacher is asking students to pay close attention to their word choice. What follows are a few strategies to assist students in replacing common adjectives.

1. *Banned words:* No, this is not an exercise in censorship but rather a way for teachers to literally force students into reaching for more sophisticated language. This can actually be a type of word wall; I have seen pictures of garbage cans, toilets, and tombstones used as "final resting places" for tired words such as *pretty, glad, sad,* and *mad.* As you read student writing, write the trashed, flushed, or dead words (depending on your graphic) on note cards and place them on the wall. You must then work with students to replace these words; essentially a list of words that should be used in their place.

2. *Semantic gradients* (Blachowicz & Fisher, 2006; Greenwood & Flanigan, 2007): Semantic gradients are ways for students to explore the shades of meaning and relationships of words. They can be set up in different ways, but the intent is always the same: replace common words with new words. Greenwood and Flanigan use semantic gradients for students to think of words in opposition (for example, *obese* to *skinny*). The words are set up on a scale, and students work to fill in the center of the scale with highly descriptive words. An example of this semantic gradient is in Figure 10.5.

Figure 10.5 Semantic Gradient Example

Source: Greenwood & Flanigan, 2007

In this semantic gradient, you can provide the words to be filled in (in this example, choices include *slender, thin, chubby, hefty, average*) or allow students to come up with their own words.

Another type of semantic gradient strategy is called Shades of Meaning. In this strategy, distribute paint chips to students, along with resources to look up synonyms, such as a thesaurus or a computer with access to Web sites such as thesaurus.com. (Tip: when gathering paint chips from your favorite home improvement store, let the sales associate know you are not stealing but providing a workspace for students to explore adjectives!) Students can work in pairs or individually in this strategy. Give each student a basic adjective to start with, such as *good, bad,* or *ugly.* Have the student write the word in the first color on the paint chip. Then have the student use the resources to come up with a variety of words that share this meaning, working to fill in each color on the chip with an increasingly sophisticated word. At the end, you will have paint chips ready to decorate your room with replacements for basic adjectives. During writing time, encourage students to walk to this new word wall and replace their words with sophisticated ones!

Common Core Connection

Bumping up the sophistication of language used in the classroom is reflected in the Common Core State Standards for English/Language (Figure 10.6 on page 124).

Figure 10.6 Common Core State Standards

Grade Level	4	5	6
Standard Addressed	**Language Standard** Acquire and use accurately grade-appropriate general academic and domain-specific words and phrases, including those that signal precise actions, emotions, or states of being (e.g., *quizzed, whined, stammered*) and that are basic to a particular topic (e.g., *wildlife, conservation,* and *endangered* when discussing animal preservation).	**Language Standard** Acquire and use accurately grade-appropriate general academic and domain-specific words and phrases, including those that signal contrast, addition, and other logical relation-ships (e.g., *however, although, nevertheless, similarly, moreover, in addition*).	**Language Standard** Acquire and use accurately grade-appropriate general academic and domain-specific words and phrases; gather vocabulary knowledge when considering a word or phrase important to comprehension or expression.
Grade Level	**7**	**8**	**9–10**
Standard Addressed	**Language Standard** Acquire and use accurately grade-appropriate general academic and domain-specific words and phrases; gather vocabulary knowledge when considering a word or phrase important to comprehension or expression.	**Language Standard** Acquire and use accurately grade-appropriate general academic and domain-specific words and phrases; gather vocabulary knowledge when considering a word or phrase important to comprehension or expression.	**Language Standard** Acquire and use accurately general academic and domain-specific words and phrases, sufficient for read-ing, writing, speak-ing, and listening at the college and career readiness level; demonstrate independence in gathering vocabu-lary knowledge when considering a word or phrase important to comprehension or expression.

Source: NGAC/CCSSO, 2010

Action Steps

Modeling and encouraging the use of academic language in the classroom is not only imperative to building vocabularies, but also fun! Take some action:

1. Talk with your colleagues about building an atmosphere that welcomes and encourages academic language in your building.

   a. What actions could you take to build this atmosphere?

   _____

   _____

   b. What could different teachers/teams contribute to make academic language the norm?

   _____

   _____

2. Select a semantic gradient activity to complete with your students—either the antonym or the paint chip activity.

   a. Which did you choose? Why?

   b. After implementing this activity, REFLECT: How do you think you can encourage students to continue to improve their use of sophisticated language in their writing?

   _____

   _____

   _____

   _____

Knowledge Ratings Chart

Name: _____

Vocabulary	I know this	I've seen or heard this	Have No Idea	Prove It!
1.				
2.				
3.				
4.				
5.				
6.				
7.				

References

Allen, J. (2007). *Inside words: Tools for teaching academic vocabulary, grades 4–12*. New York, NY: Stenhouse.

Allen, J. (2010). Steps for teaching vocabulary. Paper presented at the *National Middle School Association Conference*, Baltimore, MD.

Allington, R. (2002). What I've learned about effective reading instruction. *Phi Delta Kappan, 83*, 740-747.

Allington, R., & Cunningham, P. (2006). *Schools that work: Where all children read and write* (3rd ed.). Boston, MA: Allyn & Bacon.

Barger, J. (2006). Building word consciousness. *The Reading Teacher, 60*(3), 279–281.

Baumann, J., Edwards, E., Boland, E., Olejnik, S., & Kame'enui, E. (2003). Vocabulary tricks: Effects of instruction in morphology and context on fifth-grade students' ability to derive and infer word meanings. *American Educational Research Journal, 40*, 447–494.

Baumann, J. F., Kame'enui, E. J., & Ash, G. E. (2003). Research on vocabulary instruction: Voltaire redux. In J. Flood, D. Lapp, J. R. Squire, & J. M. Jensen (Eds.), *Handbook of research on teaching the English language arts* (2nd ed., pp. 752–785). Mahwah, NJ: Erlbaum.

Beck, I. L., McKeown, M. G., & Kucan, L. (2002). *Bringing words to life: Robust vocabulary instruction.* NY: Guilford.

Beers, K. (2002). *When kids can't read—what teachers can do: A guide for teachers 6-12.* Portsmouth, NH: Heinemann.

Blachowicz, C. L. Z., Fisher, P. J. (2006). *Teaching vocabulary in all classrooms.* Upper Saddle NJ: Pearson Education.

Bromley, K. (2003). Round-the-clock vocabulary. *Instructor, 113*, 29–31.

Bromley, K. (2007). Nine things every teacher should know about vocabulary instruction. *Journal of Adolescent and Adult Literacy, 50*, 528–537.

Brown, M. W. (1990). *The Important Book.* New York, NY: HarperCollins.

Callella, T. (2001). *Making your word wall more interactive.* Huntington Beach, CA: Creative Teaching Press.

Clementi, L. B. (2010). Readers Theater. *Phi Delta Kappan, 91*(5), 85–88.

Collins, S. (2008). *The Hunger Games.* New York, NY: Scholastic.

Dietz, F., Hofer, M., & Fries, S. (2007). Individual values, learning routines, and academic procrastination. *British Journal of Educational Psychology, 77*, 893–906.

Fisher, D., Brozo, W., Frey, N., & Ivey, G. (2011). *50 instructional routines to develop content literacy*. Boston, MA: Pearson.

Fisher, D., & Frey, N. (2008). *Word wise and content rich, grades 7–12*. Portsmouth, NH: Heinemann.

Fisher, D., & Frey, N. (2011). *Improving adolescent literacy: Content area strategies at work* (3rd ed.). Boston, MA: Allyn & Bacon.

Gallagher, K. (2009). *Readicide: How schools are killing reading and what you can do about it*. Portland, ME: Stenhouse.

Graves, M., & Watts-Taffe, S. (2008). For the love of words: Fostering word consciousness in young readers. *The Reading Teacher, 62*, 185–193.

Greenwood, S.C., & Flanigan, K. (2007). Overlapping vocabulary and comprehension: Context clues complement semantic gradients. *The Reading Teacher, 61*, 249–254.

Grimes, P. (2009). Connecting adolescents with text: Word walls to boost content comprehension. *The Virginia English Bulletin, 59*, 39–43.

Harmon, J., Wood, J., Hedrick, W., Vintinner, J., & Willeford, T. (2009). Interactive word walls: more than just writing on the walls. *Journal of Adolescence and Adult Literacy, 52*, 398–408.

Harmon, J., Wood, K., & Kiser, K. (2009). Promoting vocabulary learning with the interactive word wall. *Middle School Journal, 40*, 58-63.

Ivey, G., & Broaddus, K. (2007). A formative experiment investigating literacy engagement among Latina/o students just beginning to read, write, and speak English. *Reading Research Quarterly, 42*, 512–545.

Ivey, G., & Fisher, D. (2005). Learning from what doesn't work. *Educational Leadership, 63*(2), 8–15.

Jackson, J., Tripp, S., & Cox, K. (2011). Interactive word walls: Transforming content vocabulary instruction. *Science Scope*, 45–49.

Keehn, S., Harmon, J., & Shoho, A. (2008). Issues of fluency, comprehension, and vocabulary. *Reading and Writing Quarterly, 24*(4), 335–362.

Ketterlin-Geller, L., McCoy, J., Twynman, T., & Tindal, G. (2006). Using a concept maze to assess student understanding of secondary content. *Assessment for Effective Intervention, 32*, 39–50.

Klinger, J., Vaughn, S., & Boardman, A. (2007). *Teaching reading comprehension to students with learning difficulties*. New York, NY: Guilford Press.

Krashen, Stephen D (1993). *The Power of Reading: Insights from the research*. New York, NY: Libraries Unlimited.

Lane, H., & Allen, S. (2010). The vocabulary-rich classroom: Modeling sophisticated word use to promote word consciousness and vocabulary growth. *The Reading Teacher, 63*, 363–370.

Lapp, D., Fisher, D., & Jacobson, J. (2008). Useful instructional routines for adolescent English language learner' vocabulary development. *The California Reader, 42*, 10–22.

Lowry, Lois. (2002). *The Giver*. New York, NY: Laurel Leaf.

Lynch, J. (2005). *The Highest Tide*. New York, NY: Bloomsbury.

Marzano, R. (2004). *Classroom instruction that works: Research-based strategies for increasing student achievement*. New York, NY: Prentice Hall.

Marzano, R. J. (2010). Representing knowledge nonlinguistically. *Educational Leadership, 67*, 84–86.

McKenna, M., & Robinson, R. (2009). *Teaching through text: Reading and writing in the content areas.* Boston, MA: Pearson.

McLaughlin, M. (2010). *Content area reading: Teaching and learning in an age of multiple literacies.* Boston, MA: Pearson.

McLaughlin, M., & Allen, M. B. (2002). *Guided Comprehension: A teaching model for grades 3–8.* Newark, DE: International Reading Association.

Miller, M., & Veatch, N. (2011). *Literacy in context (LinC): Choosing instructional strategies to teach reading in content areas for students in grades 5–12.* Boston, MA: Pearson.

Nagy, W., & Anderson, R. (1984). How many words are there in printed school English? *Reading Research Quarterly, 19*, 303–330.

Nagy, W. (1988). *Teaching vocabulary to improve reading comprehension.* Urbana, IL: National Council of Teachers of English.

Nagy, W. (October 2008). *Choosing words to teach: Beyond Tier Two.* Paper presented at the meeting of International Reading Association, West Regional Conference, Portland, OR.

National Governors Association for Best Practices, Council of Chief State School Officers. (2010). Common core state standards (English Language Arts). Washington, DC: Author.

Ohianan, S. (2006). Taking a look at a few sacred cows in teaching vocabulary. *The NERA Journal, 42*, 12–18.

Payne, R. (2005). *A framework for understanding poverty.* Highlands, TX: aha! Process, Inc.

Pearson, P., Hiebert, E., & Kamil, M. (2007). Vocabulary assessment: What we know and what we need to learn. *Reading Research Quarterly, 42*, 282–296.

Rasinski, T. (2003). *The fluent reader: Oral reading strategies for building word recognition, fluency, and comprehension.* New York, NY: Scholastic.

Rasinski, T., & Padak, N. (2000). Effective reading strategies (2nd ed.). Upper Saddle River, NJ: Prentice Hall.

Rasinski, T., Padak, N., Newton, J., & Newton, E. (2010). The Latin-Greek connection: Building vocabulary through morphological study. *The Reading Teacher, 65*, 133–141.

Routman, R. (2002). *Reading essentials: The specifics you need to teach reading well.* Portsmouth, NH: Heinemann.

Scott, J. A., Jamieson-Noel, D., & Asselin, M. (2003). Vocabulary instruction throughout the day in 23 Canadian upper-elementary classrooms. *Elementary School Journal, 103*, 269–268.

Scott, J. A., & Nagy, W. E. (1997). Understanding the definitions of unfamiliar words. *Reading Research Quarterly, 32*, 184–200.

Stahl, K., & Bravo, M. (2010). Contemporary classroom vocabulary assessment for content areas. *The Reading Teacher, 63*, 566–578.

Taba, H. (1967). Teacher's handbook for elementary social studies. Reading, MA: Addison-Wesley.

Tierney, R. J., & Readence, J. E. (2000). *Reading strategies and practices: A compendium* (5th ed.). Boston, MA: Allyn & Bacon.

Tortello, R. (2004). Tableaux vivants in the literature classroom. *The Reading Teacher, 58*(2), 206–208.

Tunkel, T. (2012). Word wall use in our kindergarten classroom. *Retrieved from* http://www.calicocookie.com/wordwall.html.

Vacca, J., Vacca, R., Gove, M., Burkey, L. C., Lenhart, L. A., & McKeon, C. (2011). *Reading and learning to read* (8th ed.). Boston, MA: Allyn & Bacon.

Vacca, R., Vacca, J., & Mraz, M. (2011). *Content area reading: Literacy and learning across the curriculum* (10th ed.). New York, NY: Pearson.

Vallejo, B. (2006). Word wall. *The Science Teacher, 73*, 58–60.

Wiggins, G., & McTighe, J. (2005). *Understanding by design.* Alexandria, VA: ASCD.

Wilfong, L. (2012). The science text for all: Using Textmasters to help all students access written science content. *Science Scope, 46*–53.

Wilhelm, J. (2002). *Action strategies for deepening comprehension: Using drama strategies to assist reading performance.* New York, NY: Scholastic.

Yates, P., Cuthrell, K., & Rose, M. (2011). Out of the room and into the hall: Making content word walls work. *The Clearing House, 84*, 31–36.